MONDAY MOTIVATION WITH 101 REFLECTIONS

BHAWNA AGRAWAL

An imprint of
Srishti Publishers & Distributors

Srishti Publishers & Distributors
A unit of AJR Publishing LLP
212A, Peacock Lane
Shahpur Jat, New Delhi – 110 049

editorial@srishtipublishers.com

First published by Bold,
An imprint of Srishti Publishers & Distributors in 2026

10 9 8 7 6 5 4 3 2

This is a work of non-fiction, based on the authors' experiences and life-learnings. It provides practical solutions to everyday problems, but the recommendations given herein are in no way intended to be a substitute for professional advice and help. The stories inside the book are taken from various open sources and neither the author, nor the publisher claim any rights to the stories.

Printed and bound in India.

Dedicated to our beloved friend, philosopher, and guide, *Param Pujya Pappaji*. Thank you for illuminating the lives of all those fortunate enough to have crossed paths with you.

Foreword

It is a true joy to write the foreword for *Monday Motivation with 101 Reflections*, a collection of 101 tales that arrives like a gentle light at the beginning of each week.

Mondays often symbolize a new beginning, a fresh start, renewed responsibilities, and quiet aspirations waiting to be fulfilled. In offering the reflections of the tales, Bhawna transforms Monday from a routine marker of time into a divine opportunity which takes a moment to realign, reflect, and reconnect with purpose.

Each story in this collection carries a simple yet powerful message. They remind us that growth is not always found in grand events but in small awakenings. Week after week, lives have quietly transformed, comfort zones broken and dreams revived. They gently encourage us to lead with compassion, resilience, and gratitude.

What makes this book special is its accessibility. The tales are easy to read yet profound in meaning. They speak to people from all walks of life, whether one is at the beginning of a journey, in the midst of challenges, or quietly seeking deeper understanding.

In a world filled with constant noise, *Monday Motivation* offers stillness. In times of uncertainty, it offers oneself to be grounded. The tales are simple but motivates us and offers reassurance of divine wisdom.

I commend Bhawna for bringing together these reflections with sincerity and devotion. May this book become a weekly companion for many, a source of renewed clarity, courage, and spiritual strength.

With blessings for the author and every reader who turns these pages,

With grace and warm regards,

—Paresh Shah
CEO, Sapna Book House (P) Limited

Acknowledgements

Some books are written out of passion, some from knowledge, some from faith, and this one is a pure blessing bestowed upon me by my guardian angels.

Somehow, I am lucky enough to be the name behind the book, but there are hands, minds, and intentions that curated it with me, and I extend my deepest gratitude to each one of them.

I start by thanking my friend, Achira Mehta, for planting the seed of the idea for this anthology to be a handbook of inspiration and motivation for everyday life struggles and doubts.

I am grateful to the SRATRC team, led by Reshma Dhami, for tirelessly and consistently sharing the Monday motivation stories and ensuring that they are the first thing in our inbox every Monday morning.

I thank my team member, Shubhi Jain, and my editor, Surbhi Jalan Gupta, who sat with me for hours on end, conceptualizing and brainstorming the layout of the book, and making sure that the work kept going despite many ups and downs in the journey of this book.

To Yash, the hero of my life, thank you for always being there and telling me, "You go ahead, I will take care of everything," which gives me the confidence to think the unthinkable.

To my kids, Avyukt and Ihra, for being my cheerleaders and the wonderful little humans who are the testimony of the incredible impact these stories have.

I also extend my gratitude to my mentor for life, Pujya Nilesh *bhai*, who has always guided, supported, and encouraged me to go ahead, and that's how this book became possible.

And finally, to my friend, philosopher, and guide, Param Pujya Pappaji. Everything good in my life, work, and existence is only and only because of his unconditional love and blessings.

A Story

Once upon a time, there was a story...a story woven with threads of wisdom into beautiful patterns, with such eloquently colourful words and the unique design of emotions that whoever listened to it or read it—with the right heart—learnt from it, and whoever retold it gained a new perspective each time it was repeated...

Soon, it had been retold countless times, in many languages and in various versions, destined to live on forever.

Why This Book?

We are a sum total of our surroundings—sounds, visuals, words, people, thoughts, and everything we can think of—that have shaped and continue to shape us in some way or another. It is rightly said that our consumption directly reflects in our personality, which is not just the food we consume but also our thoughts, behaviour, and words.

Our approach and perspective in life are directly influenced by the conversations we engage in or are exposed to. In the present times, when we are living the most comfortable lives in the history of mankind, little discomfort unsettles us; we are quick to deem a bad day as a bad life altogether and, through our unconscious actions, ensure that we remain unhappy.

Imagine what social media culture has presented us with. Right at the beginning of the weekend, we are inundated with memes that are critical of the approaching Monday. We are so busy brooding over the tasks awaiting us on Monday and lamenting the upcoming workweek that we forget to enjoy the weekend. Starting on a resentful note is what creates the blues.

Here is a book that strives to turn this around. Let's begin with the motivation that keeps us going and helps us enjoy our work and life. These 101 stories will nudge you to be grateful and look forward to the wonderful gift we call LIFE!

This book can serve as:

- A motivational start to the day;
- A repository of heartwarming short stories;
- A positive nudge before going to bed;
- A tool for instilling the right values in children; and
- A detox from aimless digital scrolling.

Often, we find that we have the resources but lack the knowledge of "how to judiciously use those resources". Therefore, here are a few points for you to remember while reading and using this book as a tool to change "how you look at life":

- This book contains 101 short stories classified under various themes.
- Each day presents a different experience or challenge, and you are free to choose the theme or story that resonates most with you on that day.
- Every theme includes some questions to ponder, and we request that you not skip these questions.
- You may begin your day with this book and use these reflection questions as prompts for your journal.
- Read the story and try to apply the learnings.
- Each story can offer one or multiple takeaways, and you should note your key insights in the space provided.

The Pencil Story

A boy was watching his grandmother write a letter.

After a while, he asked, "Are you writing a story about what we have done? Is it a story about me?"

His grandmother stopped writing and replied, "Yes, I am writing about you, but more important than the words is the pencil I am using. I hope you will be like this pencil when you grow up."

Intrigued, the boy looked at the pencil. It didn't seem special in any way, and he quipped, "But it seems like any other pencil I have ever seen!"

The grandmother was quick to respond. "That depends on how you view things," she said. "This pencil has five qualities, which, if you manage to hold onto, will make you a person who is always at peace with the world.

"First quality: You are capable of great things, but you should never forget that there is a guiding hand behind your steps. We call that hand God, and He always guides us according to His will.

"Second quality: Every now and then, I have to stop writing and use a sharpener. That causes the pencil to suffer, but afterwards, it becomes much sharper. So you, too, must learn to bear certain pains and sorrows because they will make you a better person.

"Third quality: The pencil always allows us to use an eraser to rub out any mistakes. This means that correcting what we have done is not necessarily a bad thing; it helps us stay on the path of justice.

"Fourth quality: What truly matters in a pencil is not its wooden exterior but the graphite inside. So always remember to pay attention to what is happening inside you.

"Finally, the pencil's fifth quality: It always leaves a mark. In the same way, you should know that everything you do in life will leave a mark, so try to be conscious of that in every action."

Be the Pencil.

PERSPECTIVE

What Do You Choose to See?
Perception is the key! How you perceive the world, people, situations, and circumstances determines what the world has to offer you...

1. Have you wondered why the same boiling water that hardens an egg softens a potato?
2. Imagine you work for a shoe manufacturing company and are sent to a remote island to create a market. To your surprise, nobody on that island wears any footwear—no concept of footwear at all. What will be your reaction?

1. Point of View

Once there was a little boy named Andy. He was a cheerful ball of energy with a curious mind. It was time for the school's Annual Day, and he was asked to audition with his classmates for a part in the school play. His mother knew he was eager to be in the play, and she was worried about how he would react if he wasn't chosen.

On the day the parts were given out, Andy's mother went to pick him up from school, feeling anxious about the outcome.

Seeing his mother, Andy rushed to her, his eyes shining with pride and excitement.

"Guess what, Mum," he shouted, then said the words that can provide a lesson to us all, "I've been chosen to clap and cheer."

His mother was surprised and speechless for a moment, but her heart was full to see her boy viewing life with such optimism, a perspective many of us fail to adopt.

Gaining a different point of view can lead to new and unexpected insights.

2. Is it that Difficult to Highlight Strengths?

Once, a king with a defect in one eye and one leg wanted his portrait to be painted, one that would make him look perfect. He ordered all the painters to do so. The painters were at a loss and held long discussions and brainstorming sessions, but no one dared to draw the king with his imperfections, as none could think of a way to portray him as beautiful despite his flaws.

One painter finally agreed and created a masterpiece. He displayed it before a crowd of 1500 citizens, and everyone was awestruck.

The painting depicted the king aiming for a hunt, with one eye closed and a leg bent for stability!

Why can't we all paint others this way—hiding their weaknesses and highlighting their strengths?

May we, too, be blessed with the wisdom to hide others' weaknesses and bring their virtues to light.

3. The Wonderful Mess

A renowned business tycoon, known for several major breakthroughs, was being interviewed. The reporter asked what made him more creative than others. He smiled and recounted a personal experience.

When he was a little boy, he had tried to remove a bottle of milk from the refrigerator but lost his grip and dropped the bottle, spilling milk all over.

His mother entered the kitchen, and instead of scolding or punishing him, she said, "Ankush, what a great and wonderful mess you have made! I have rarely seen such a huge puddle of milk. Well, the damage is done. Would you like to play in the milk for a few minutes before we clean it up?"

He did. After a few minutes, his mother said, "Ankush, whenever you make a mess, eventually you have to clean it up and restore everything to its proper order. How would you like to do that? We could use a sponge, a towel, or a mop. Which do you prefer?"

He chose the sponge, and together they cleaned up the spilt milk. His mother then said, "You know, what we have here is a failed experiment in how to carry a big milk bottle with two tiny hands. Let's go out in the backyard and fill the bottle with water to see if you can find a way to carry it without dropping it." The little boy learned that if he grasped the bottle at the mouth with both hands, he could carry it safely. What a wonderful lesson!

He then remarked to the reporter that it was at that moment he realized that experimenting, making mistakes, and taking chances are ongoing processes to discovering better and quicker ways to do things. His mother turned a failure into a positive lesson, inspiring him to find creative solutions to his problems.

How we handle failure and missed opportunities reveals much about us—both professionally and personally. Searching for the silver lining amid dark clouds is perhaps one of the most important ways in which we can motivate ourselves instead of resigning to despair.

Let us focus on that silver lining.

4. The Flowers of Lanka

The great saint Samartha Guru Ramadas, the Guru of Shivaji, was composing the epic Ramayana. He reached the part where Hanuman reached Lanka in search of Sita. He wrote, "Hanuman, the brave messenger of Lord Rama, searched the entire city of Lanka to find Sita. Lanka was full of mesmerizingly lush and colourful gardens. He searched through the palace and the gardens. There were white flowers blooming all over the garden." Just then, a sharp voice reprimanded him, "No! That is wrong!"

Ramadas looked up from his work and was surprised to see Hanuman standing before him. Hanuman said, "I have been hovering around you many times, enjoying your composition of the Ramayana, but what you just recited is incorrect."

Ramadas said humbly, "My Lord, I don't understand. What is wrong with it?"

Hanuman quickly replied, "Lanka was certainly full of flowers, but they were red in colour. They were not white as you have written. So I want you to correct it."

Ramadas humbly folded his hands and said, "Oh, Anjaneya! Lord Rama would never put the wrong words into my mind. I am writing exactly what He is guiding me to write. I have not seen the flowers."

Hanuman insisted, "You are writing what you see through your mind's eye. I am telling you what I actually witnessed with my own eyes. Let me tell you once and for all, the flowers in Lanka were red and only RED."

Ramadas said, "I'm sorry, but my Lord Rama instructs me to write that the flowers were white. Perhaps you were mistaken, or perhaps you have forgotten."

Just then, there was a flash of blinding white light.

Wonder of wonders! Lord Rama appeared out of nowhere! Hanuman was the first to prostrate himself at His beloved Lord's feet. Ramadas followed suit.

Hanuman was quick to say, "Oh, Lord! Thank you for coming, for we are unable to resolve a dispute."

Lord Rama smiled benevolently and said, "Hanuman, what Ramadas is seeing through his mind's eye is correct. Lanka was indeed full of white flowers!"

Hanuman was dumbstruck. "But, my Lord, what about the red flowers that I saw?"

Rama smiled again and continued, "That, too, was true, my dearest one. At that time, you were looking for Sita. Your eyes were red with anger. So the white flowers appeared red to you!"

Hanuman bowed before his master, and Lord Rama continued, "Hanuman, all that we see around us in the world appears to us in accordance with our attitude or the condition of our mind. The world is but a mirror of what we are. If we are happy, the world seems to be a happy place. If we are sad, even the trees and the flowers appear to be sad and drooping."

It is always about how you see it!

5. Blessing in Disguise

There was a breakfast point near a cluster of factories. Workers from these factories often went there for breakfast, and during peak hours, it was always very busy. Sunil, the floor shop manager from one of these factories, was also a frequent visitor to this breakfast point. He had often noticed that a particular person would come and take advantage of the crowd, eating and then secretly leaving without paying.

One day, while he was eating, Sunil discreetly informed the owner of the breakfast point that this person was exploiting the rush and leaving without settling the bill. The owner listened carefully and smiled, telling Sunil to let him go without saying anything and that they would discuss it later.

The next time Sunil visited the breakfast place, as usual, he saw the fellow quietly slipping away without paying the bill. After he left, Sunil asked the owner why he had been ignoring this man's actions. The owner's answer baffled Sunil.

The owner told Sunil that he was not the only one to have noticed the man; many others had seen him as well. In fact, the owner himself also knew that this person would wait in front of the eatery till it was crowded, and then he would sneak in and eat. However, the owner always ignored it and never stopped him, caught him, or tried to humiliate him. It was the owner's belief that the rush in his shop was due to the prayers of this man—he would be sitting in front of the shop, praying for it to become busy so that he could quickly go in, eat, and leave.

The owner did not want to invite misfortune by cutting his own leg in the matter of this prayer between the man and the Divine.

Each one of us has earned such blessings in disguise. All we need to recognize them is a little change in our perspective.

6. The Catholic and the Muslim

Once, in a big gathering, a Catholic priest and a young Muslim man were sitting together during lunch. When the waiter came by with a tray, everyone helped themselves, except the Muslim, who was observing the annual fast prescribed by the Koran. When lunch was over, and people were leaving, a guest remarked, "Do you see how fanatical these Muslims are? I'm glad to see you Catholics aren't like them."

"But we are," said the priest. "He is trying to serve God, just as I am. We merely follow different laws." He then added, "It's a shame that people see only the differences that separate them. If they were to look at others with more love, they would mainly see what all individuals have in common, and then half the world's problems would be solved!"

Everything changes when you change your point of focus.

7. Buddha and the Angry King

Once, a king was getting ready for the evening Town-hall meeting. Hundreds of people would gather to receive help, updates, and instructions from the king. When he reached the hall, he was puzzled to find hardly a dozen people present.

He enquired about the others. One of his ministers replied, "They have all gone to see Buddha." This angered the king, and he ordered his charioteer to take him to the location.

On reaching, he stepped down from the chariot and went straight to Buddha. "Who are you? What are you doing here in my territory?" he thundered. "Are you a king or a merchant? You look like a beggar to me, who himself is dependent on others to survive."

The king paused for breath, then continued, "If these people need food, medicine, shelter, livelihood, or relief of any kind, I am the one who helps them. What have you done for them? What have you given them? Nothing, it seems. Then why do all these people flock to you?"

Buddha looked at the king and gently pulled off the silk scarf he was wearing on his shoulders. He asked, "Dear King, this cloth is very beautiful. What is it called?"

The king replied, "It's a scarf."

After a moment, Buddha started tying knots in the scarf and then asked the king, "What do you see now?"

The king replied, "Knots."

Buddha answered very gently, "My dear king, you help people, but you help them by looking at their knots, whereas I still see the scarf. That makes all the difference!"

All that makes a difference is how you see something!

ACTION TIME

1. How do you feel about the stories?
2. What are your learnings?
3. What things will you do differently from now on and how?

(Please refer to the stories if needed.)

List some challenges or problems that you have faced in your life.

____
____
____

Now revisit each of these episodes of your life and analyze how it has changed you for the better or helped you expand your comfort zone.

____
____
____

Remember: The best way to check whether or not a particular perspective is the right one is by asking yourself: “When I look at it this way, am I growing or shrinking as a human being?”

SELF-BELIEF

Everything is possible for the one who believes!
You are your only limit!
If you think YOU CAN, YOU CAN!
If you think YOU CAN'T, YOU CAN'T!
Read that again.
It's YOU who decides your limits, nobody else.

1. Do you know that a bumblebee cannot fly? It is too heavy for its tiny wings to make flight possible. However, here is the twist to the tale. The bumblebee doesn't know this, and so, it flies! What does this tell you?
2. Have you tried something you initially thought was not your cup of tea but then realized you did quite well at it?

8. Do You Know Your Best Move?

A 10-year-old boy decided to learn judo despite losing his left arm in a devastating car accident. He began training under an old Japanese judo master and, surprisingly, was doing well. One thing that bothered the boy was that even after three months of training, the master had taught him only one move.

Finally, one day, the boy asked his master, "Sensei, shouldn't I be learning more moves?"

"This is the only move you'll ever need to know," the sensei replied.

The boy couldn't understand what his master meant, but believing in his teacher, he continued training. Several months later, the sensei took the boy to his first tournament. The boy was surprised at how easily he won his first two matches.

The third match proved to be more difficult. After some time, his opponent became impatient and charged, but the boy deftly used his one move to win the match. The young boy was amazed at his success and was now in the finals. This time, his opponent was bigger, stronger, and more experienced. For a while, the boy appeared to be over-matched. Concerned that the boy might get hurt, the referee called for a time-out. He was about to stop the match when the sensei intervened. "No," the sensei insisted, "let him continue."

Soon after the match resumed, the boy's opponent made a critical mistake: he dropped his guard. Instantly, the boy used his move to pin him.

The boy won the match and the tournament. He was declared the champion. On their way home, the boy and the sensei reviewed every move in each match. Then the boy mustered the courage to ask what was truly on his mind. "Sensei, how did I win the tournament with only one move?"

"You won for two reasons," the sensei answered. "First, you've almost mastered one of the most difficult throws in judo. And second, the only known defence for that move is for your opponent to grab your left arm."

The boy's biggest weakness had become his biggest strength.

Sometimes we feel we have certain weaknesses and blame God, circumstances, and ourselves for them, but we don't know that our weaknesses can become our strength one day.

Hone your strengths and embrace your weaknesses.
Believe in yourself!

9. The Sun and the Cave

One day, the sun and a cave struck up a conversation. The sun had trouble understanding what "dark" meant, while the cave couldn't comprehend the meaning of "light and clear". So, they decided to exchange places.

The cave went up to the sun and said, "Ah, I see! This is beyond wonderful! Now come down and see where I have been living."

The sun went down to the cave and said, "I don't see any difference." This was so because when the sun went down, it took its light along with it, and even the darkest corners were illuminated.

We believe that heaven is a place where we should go, little realizing it is our state of mind which creates heaven or hell.

If you are full of darkness, negativity, fear, and doubt, you become a cave unknowingly. It's hell within, and no matter how many material comforts you accumulate, you still remain hollow.

On the other hand, if you are illuminated like the sun, then the darkness of the cave wouldn't matter. Even in the worst of circumstances, you will still be able to find a blessing somewhere.

The enlightened ones can never be sent to hell or pushed into darkness. They carry their heaven on their shoulders all the time. Let us start carrying our heaven within us.

Moksha is a state of the soul.

10. All Power is Within You

Once in a village, there were two young best friends. On a bright Sunday morning, while they were playing far away from the village, one of them, who was 10 years old, fell into a well. He didn't know how to swim and started shouting for help. The other friend, who was 6 years old, was a thin and frail boy. He was petrified after seeing his friend fall.

He looked around frantically for someone or something to help his friend, but all he could find was a rope tied to a bucket. He threw it down the well and used his full strength to pull his friend out. His hands were red and bruised, his feet were wobbly from holding onto the ground really tight, but he didn't loosen his hold until he saved his friend.

They were afraid to tell anyone about this incident in the village for fear of being punished. However, they decided to share it with their parents, who, surprisingly, did not believe them. In fact, when others came to know of it, no one believed them. How could a thin 6-year-old boy pull a 10-year-old out of a well?

The villagers shared the incident with a wise old man of the village. "How can a 6-year-old achieve such a feat?" they asked.

He smiled and replied, "It's simple, just like the boys told you—he threw the rope and pulled him out."

The villagers quipped, "How is that possible? How could he do it?

The wise man said, "He could do so because at the time he helped him, there was no one around to tell him he could not do it."

Your limits lie in the mind. All power is within you. If you decide something is possible and can happen, no one can stop you.

When you decide that you can, you will!

11. Walking On Water

Once there was a boy who lived with his family on a farm. They had a beautiful dog that would go down to the pond near their house for hours every day in the spring and summer with the boy to practise retrieving various items. The boy wanted to prepare his dog for duck season because he wanted him to be the best hunting dog in the entire county.

Regular vigorous training sessions made the dog so obedient that he wouldn't do anything unless told to do so by the boy. As duck season rolled in with the fall and winter months, the boy and his dog eagerly went to their regular spot down at the pond. Only a few minutes passed before the two heard the first flock of ducks flying overhead. The boy slowly raised his gun and shot three times before killing a duck, which landed in the centre of the pond. When the boy signalled his dog to retrieve the duck, the latter charged towards it into the pond. However, instead of swimming in the water like he had practised so many times, the dog walked on the water's surface, retrieved the duck, and returned to the boy.

The boy was astonished. His dog could walk on water! It was magic!

The boy knew no one would ever believe the amazing thing he had just witnessed. He had to get someone else down there to witness this incredible spectacle.

The boy went to a nearby farmer's house and asked if he would hunt with him the next morning. The neighbour agreed and met the boy the following morning at his regular spot by the pond. The pair patiently waited for a flock of ducks to fly overhead, and soon enough, they heard them coming. The boy told the neighbour to take a shot, which he did, killing one duck. Just as the day before, the boy signalled his dog to fetch the duck. Miraculously, the dog walked on the water again to retrieve the duck.

The boy was bursting with pride and could hardly contain himself as he asked his neighbour, "Did you see that? What do you think?"

The neighbour responded, "I wasn't going to say anything, but your dog doesn't even know how to swim."

The boy sat stunned as his neighbour pointed out a potential flaw in the dog rather than recognizing that what he had just done was a miracle.

People will often downplay others' abilities or achievements because they're unable to accomplish the same. Don't let this dishearten you. Just move on and keep working on improving yourself. Maintaining a positive mindset is an essential part of being successful.

Furthermore, be conscious of instances where you may be tempted to not give credit where it is deserved. Highlighting other people's shortcomings does not make you superior to them.

Each person will evaluate your worth based on their own capabilities, knowledge, and values. Only a jeweller knows the true worth of a diamond!

12. Keep Your Dream

Jack had a friend named Monty Roberts who owned a horse ranch in San Ysidro. He let Jack use his house to host fund-raising events to raise money for youth-at-risk programmes. Once, Monty introduced Jack, saying, "I want to tell you why I let Jack use my house. It all goes back to a story about a young man whose father was an itinerant horse trainer who would go from stable to stable, race track to race track, farm to farm, and ranch to ranch, training horses. As a result, the boy's high school education was continually interrupted. When he was a senior, he was asked to write a paper about what he wanted to be and do when he grew up."

"That night, he wrote a seven-page paper describing his goal of owning a horse ranch someday. He wrote about his dream in great detail and even drew a diagram of a 200-acre ranch, showing the location of all the buildings, the stables, and the track. Then he drew a detailed floor plan for a 4,000- square-foot house that would sit on this 200-acre dream ranch."

"He put a great deal of his heart into the project and handed it in to his teacher the next day. Two days later, he received his paper back. On the front page, a large red 'FAIL' was written with a note that read, 'See me after class.' The boy went to see the teacher after class and asked, 'Why did I receive a FAIL?'"

"The teacher replied, 'This is an unrealistic dream for a young boy like you. You have no money or resources. You come from an itinerant family. Owning a horse ranch requires a lot of money. You have to buy the land, pay for the original breeding stock, and later, pay large stud fees. There's no way you could ever do it.' Then the teacher added, 'If you rewrite this paper with a more realistic goal, I will reconsider your grade.'"

"The boy went home and thought about it long and hard. He asked his father what he should do. His father said, 'Look, son, you have to make up your own mind on this. I think it is a very important decision for you.' Finally, after pondering it for a week, the boy turned in the same paper without making any changes at all. He said to his teacher, **'You can keep the FAIL, and I'll keep my dream.'"**

Monty then turned to the assembled group and said, "I tell you this story because you are sitting in my 4,000-square-foot house in the middle of my 200-acre horse ranch. I still have that school paper framed over the fireplace."

He added, "The best part of the story is that two summers ago, the same school teacher brought 30 kids to camp out on my ranch for a week. When the teacher was leaving, he said, 'Monty, I can tell you this now. When I was your teacher, I was something of a dream-stealer. During those years, I stole many children's dreams. Fortunately, you had enough gumption not to give up on yours.'"

Don't let anyone steal your dreams. Follow your heart, no matter what.

ACTION TIME

1. How do you feel about the stories?
2. What are your learnings?
3. What things will you do differently from now on and how?

(Please refer to the stories if needed.)

Who were you before the world told you who you should be? What lights your fire?

____

____

____

What are your aspirations, goals, and objectives?

____

____

____

PAUSE

It's vital to stop and smell the roses. If we are constantly running, we would certainly reach life's finish line, but we wouldn't have lived.

Only when things settle will we be able to see them clearly for what they are.

A calm mind is our ultimate weapon against all challenges.

We rarely take the time to live and enjoy the present; instead, we often find ourselves either lamenting the past or worrying about the future, squandering the precious now!

1. Make a conscious effort to live in the 'Now Moment' for a day. Don't regret what happened yesterday or stress over what might go wrong tomorrow. Instead, make a list of the things that are right today, the things that you are grateful for today.

13. Rest the Unrest

One day, a disciple and his teacher were walking through a forest. The disciple was disturbed by the fact that his mind was in a state of constant unrest.

He asked his teacher, "Why are most people's minds restless, and only a few possess a calm mind? What can one do to still the mind?"

The teacher looked at the disciple, smiled, and replied, "Let me tell you a story and see if you find your answer there."

"On a beautiful day, an elephant was standing in the shade of a tree, eating its leaves. Suddenly, a small fly came buzzing and landed on the elephant's ear. The elephant stayed calm and continued to eat, not heeding the fly."

"The fly flew around the elephant's ear, buzzing noisily, yet the elephant seemed to be unaffected. This bewildered the fly, and it asked, 'Are you deaf?'

'No,' the elephant answered.

'Why aren't you bothered by my buzz?' the fly asked.

'Why are you so restless and noisy? Why can't you stay still just for a few moments?' asked the elephant and peacefully continued eating the leaves.

The fly answered, 'Everything I see, hear, and feel attracts my attention, and all noises and movements around me affect my behaviour. What is your secret? How can you stay so calm and still?'

The elephant stopped eating and replied, 'My five senses do not disturb my peace because they do not rule my attention. I am in control of my mind and my thoughts, and therefore, I can direct my attention where I want and ignore any disturbances, including your buzz.' After a pause, the elephant continued, 'Now that I am eating, I am completely immersed in the act. In this way, I can enjoy my food and chew it better. I am in control of my attention, and therefore, I can remain peaceful.'"

Upon hearing these words, the disciple's eyes opened wide, and a smile appeared on his face.

He looked at his teacher and said gratefully, "I now understand. My mind will always be in a state of constant unrest if my five senses, and whatever is happening in the world around me, are in control of it. On the other hand, if I am in command of my five senses, able to disregard sense impressions, and able to control my thoughts, my mind will become calm, and I will be able to control its restlessness."

The teacher smiled in agreement.

Become aware of what's truly worth your energy and attention!

14. Let it Be

Once, Buddha was passing by a lake with a few of his disciples. They stopped there for a while, and Buddha told one of his disciples, "I am thirsty. Can you please get me some water from that lake?"

The disciple walked up to the lake. When he reached it, he noticed that a few people were washing clothes in the water and, right at that moment, a bullock cart began to cross through the lake.

As a result, the water became very muddy. The disciple thought, "How can I give this muddy water to Buddha to drink?" So he returned and told Buddha, "The water in there is very muddy. I don't think it is fit to drink."

After about half an hour, Buddha once again asked the same disciple to go back to the lake and get him some water to drink. The disciple obediently returned to the lake.

This time, he found that the water in the lake was absolutely clear. The mud had settled down, and the water above it looked fit to drink. So he collected some in a pot and brought it to Buddha.

Buddha looked at the water and then up at the disciple. He smiled and said, "Do you see what you did to make the water clean? You let it be. The mud settled down on its own, and you got clear water. Our minds are also the same. When it is disturbed, just let it be. Give it a little time. It will settle down on its own. You don't always have to put in effort to calm it. It will happen. It is effortless."

When you feel disturbed or unable to focus or concentrate, don't worry. Just take a deep breath and think calming thoughts. In a while, you will find a sense of calm flowing through.

Sometimes we ought to pause or even take a step back so that we can leap several steps forward.

15. Genghis Khan

One morning, the Mongol warrior, Genghis Khan, and his court went out hunting. His companions carried bows and arrows, while Genghis Khan carried on his arm his favourite falcon, which was more accurate than any arrow because it could fly up into the skies and see everything that human beings could not.

After a not very productive hunt, the Mongol warrior and his companions were on their way back when Genghis Khan felt thirsty. He luckily spotted a very thin stream of water flowing from behind a rock. He removed the falcon from his arm and took out the silver cup that he always carried with him. It took a long time to fill and, just as he was about to raise it to his lips, the falcon flew up, plucked the cup from his hands, and dashed it to the ground. Genghis Khan was furious, but then the falcon was his favourite, and perhaps it, too, was thirsty. He picked up the cup, cleaned off the dirt, and began refilling it. When the cup was only half filled, the falcon attacked it again, spilling the water.

Genghis Khan adored this bird, but he knew that he could not, under any circumstances, allow such disrespect; someone might be watching this scene from afar and, later on, might tell his warriors that the great conqueror was incapable of taming a mere bird. So, this time, he drew his sword, picked up the cup, and began to refill it, keeping one eye on the stream and the other on the falcon. As soon as he had enough water in the cup and was ready to drink, the falcon took flight again and flew towards him. Khan, with one thrust of his sword, pierced the bird's breast. The thread of water, however, had dried up, but Khan, determined now to find something to drink, climbed the rock in search of the spring. To his surprise, there was a pool of water and, in the middle of it, lay one of the most poisonous snakes in the region, dead. If he had drunk the water, he, too, would have died. Khan returned to camp with the dead falcon in his arms. He ordered a gold figurine of the bird to be prepared, and on one of the wings, he had engraved: 'Even when a friend does something you do not like, he continues to be your friend.' On the other wing, he had these words engraved: 'Any action committed in anger is an action doomed to failure.'

Any action committed in anger is an action doomed to failure.

ACTION TIME

1. How do you feel about the stories?
2. What are your learnings?
3. What things will you do differently from now on and how?

(Please refer to the stories if needed.)

Take a glass of fresh water, add some mud to it, and shake it vigorously. Can you see through the glass, or have the mud particles made the water too murky? Wait for some time, let the mud settle, and then observe. This is exactly how our minds work, too.

____

____

____

____

____

____

____

____

Allow yourself to get bored and restless, and when this feeling arises, shift your awareness to it. To start with, do this for a couple of minutes, and keep increasing the duration throughout the day.

COMPASSION

See beyond the self.
The world is a magical place; the more you take care of others, the better you are taken care of.
Putting oneself first is not selfish; only thinking about oneself all the time is.
It takes courage to put one's wishes second to other people's needs, and the reward is contentment.

1. How often do you do something for those who cannot offer you anything in return?
2. Have you ever extended a helping hand to someone in dire need and experienced the joy that comes from seeing them smile? Try experiencing it.

16. True Victory

This is a true story from a cross-country racing event held in Spain in December 2012. Kenyan champion Abel Mutai was just a few feet away from the finish line when he became confused with the signage and stopped, thinking he had completed the race.

The Spanish runner, Ivan Fernandez, was right behind him and, realizing what had happened, he shouted to the Kenyan to continue running.

Mutai didn't know Spanish and hence, couldn't understand. Comprehending this, the Spanish sprinter pushed the Kenyan champion towards the finish line, leading him to his victory.

Everyone was quite surprised at Ivan's gesture, and during the press conference, a journalist asked him why he did that.

Ivan replied, "I dream that someday we can have a kind of community where we push and help each other to win."

The journalist insisted, "But why would you let the Kenyan win?"

Ivan quickly responded, "I didn't let him win; he was going to win. The race was his."

The journalist again remarked, "But you could have won!"

Ivan looked at him and countered, "But what would be the merit of my victory? What would be the honour of that medal? How would I face myself? That victory was his; how could I take it?"

Today, Ivan Fernandez has become a hero for his honest deed that inspires integrity and the human spirit.

Victory at any cost might not always be worth it!

17. The Joy of Giving

Once upon a time, a mill owner possessed an old two-wheeler, which he had not used for a long time. Since it was becoming obsolete, the mill owner decided to resell it online and posted an advertisement, quoting its price at Rs. 30,000.

As soon as the ad was put up, he started receiving offers ranging from Rs. 15,000 to Rs. 28,000. The deals offered were great, but he thought that if people were willing to pay Rs. 28,000, someone might agree to pay Rs. 30,000 as well. The next day, he received a call from a person who offered Rs. 29,000, but he didn't confirm the deal and kept him waiting in the hope that someone would pay him Rs. 30,000.

One morning, a man called the mill owner and said, "Hello, Sir. I saw the advertisement for your moped, and I really liked it. I tried hard to earn Rs. 30,000, but have only been able to collect Rs. 24,000 until now. My son is in his final year of engineering. He has worked very hard. Sometimes he walks to his college or uses a bicycle, and sometimes he travels by bus or takes a lift from someone. I thought that at least in his final year, he should have his vehicle. I request you, Sir, to please reserve your scooter for me. A new one will cost twice as much. I would not be able to afford it at any cost. Please give me some time, and I will arrange the money." The mill owner patiently listened to him and then asked the man how he planned to arrange the remaining money. The man was silent for some time and then said, "Selling my mobile phone will also get me some money. But I pray to you, please do not sell it to anyone else."

The mill owner replied with a casual "Okay" and hung up. As

soon as he did so, a thought came to his mind, and he called the man back.

He said, "Don't sell your mobile phone. Just bring Rs. 24,000 tomorrow morning, and take the vehicle. I will sell it to you for Rs. 24,000 only."

The man on the other side could not believe his ears, and his happiness knew no bounds. He profusely thanked the mill owner and bought the scooter for Rs. 24,000 the next day.

The mill owner sold his scooter to an unknown person for Rs. 24,000, even though he had an offer of Rs. 29,000. He thought of the pleasure and joy the scooter must have brought to that family. God had been gracious and given him a lot. He realized that the biggest wealth is the ability to help someone in need.

Sometimes prioritize bringing joy to someone through your actions over your own gains.

18. Living Temple

There once lived a happy and hardworking man with his wife. He earned a livelihood by working on the land and growing crops. The couple had two sons. These two boys grew up into strong young men. They worked hard with their father, increased their land, and became well-to-do.

When the man grew very old, he said to his sons, "I may die anytime. I want you two to promise me something. After my death, both of you should always equally share the produce of this land. Never should there be any debate, argument, or fight about it."

The old man died, and the boys kept their promise to him. They always split the produce equally between themselves.

One of them got married and had five children. The other one didn't marry, but they still shared the produce equally.

One day, the unmarried brother had a worrying thought. He wondered, "My brother has a wife and five children to take care of, and I am single. Still, I take half the produce, and he takes half. This does not seem fair, but it was our father's wish. And my brother is so proud that if I try to give him some more, he will not take it. So let me do something else." Once the harvest was over, every night, he secretly carried a sack of grain on his back and put it in his brother's store.

The same concern also troubled the married brother, and he thought, "I have five boys growing up. In a few years, I will have much more happening for me, but my brother has no one. What will he do later on? He takes only 50 per cent of the produce, and I take 50 per cent. If I try to give him more, he will not take it."

He started taking one bag of grain every night and putting it in his brother's store.

A kind of reverse osmosis of grain was taking place, but neither of them realized it for a long time.

The two brothers were growing old, and they still continued to do this. One day, as both were walking with a sack of grain towards the other's store, they bumped into each other. They looked at each other and suddenly realized what had been happening all this time. They quickly averted their eyes, walked on, carried the sack of grain to its destination, returned to their houses, and slept. Time passed, and they became old and died.

The people of the town wanted to build a temple and were looking for a good site for it. After a long search, they decided the best place to build the temple was where these two brothers had met with a sack of grain on their backs, embarrassed about their own generosity.

If you live like this, you are a living temple; you do not have to worry about unconditional love, conditional love, or any of it.

Live a life that's worth emulating.

19. Fruits of Our Prayers

A voyaging ship was wrecked during a storm at sea, and only two men on it were able to swim to a small, desert-like island. The two survivors, not knowing what else to do, decided to pray to God. However, to find out whose prayers were more powerful, they agreed to divide the territory between them and stay on opposite sides of the island.

The first thing they prayed for was food. The next morning, the first man saw a fruit-bearing tree on his side of the land, and he was able to eat its fruit. The other man's parcel of land remained barren.

Soon, the first man prayed for a house, clothes, and more food. The next day, like magic, all of these were given to him. However, the second man still had nothing. Finally, the first man prayed for a ship, so that he could leave the island. In the morning, he found a ship docked at his side of the island.

The first man boarded the ship and decided to leave the second man on the island. He considered the other man unworthy to receive God's blessings, since none of his prayers had been answered.

As the ship was about to leave, the first man heard a voice from heaven, booming, "Why are you leaving your companion on the island?"

"My blessings are mine alone, since I was the one who prayed for them," the first man answered. "His prayers were all unanswered, and so he does not deserve anything."

"You are mistaken!" the voice rebuked him. "He had only one prayer, which I answered. If not for that, you would not have received any of my blessings."

"Tell me," the first man asked, "what did he pray for that I should owe him anything?"

"He prayed that all your prayers be answered."

For all we know, our blessings are not the fruits of our prayers alone, but those of another praying for us. Our prayer for you today is that all your prayers be answered. Be blessed!

What you do for others is equally important as what you do for yourself.

20. Humanity

During the reign of the great king, Obatala, three people came to his court, dragging a young man with them, and said, "O King! This man has murdered our father."

Obatala was taken aback and asked the young man, "Why did you kill their father?"

The young man replied, "I'm a goat herdsman. My goat ate from their father's farm, and he threw a stone at my goat, killing it. So, I also took the stone and threw it at their father, and he, too, died."

Obatala, on hearing the man's confession, declared, "Hearing you confess, I pass the judgement on the charge of murder and sentence you to death."

The young man pleaded, "I request three days' time before you execute the judgement. My late father left me some wealth, and I have a sister to take care of. If you kill me now, the wealth and my sister will have no guardian."

Obatala then asked, "Who will stand for your bail?" The young man, looking into the crowd, pointed at Lamurudu.

Obatala asked, "Do you agree to stand bail for him, Lamurudu?"

Lamurudu answered, "*Beeni* (yes)!"

Obatala warned, "You agree to stand for someone you don't know, but if he doesn't return, you'll receive his penalty."

Lamurudu answered, "I accept."

The young man left, but after two days, and into the third, there was still no sign of him. Everyone was very afraid for Lamurudu, who had accepted the death penalty if the man failed to return. Just before it was time for dinner, the goat herdsman appeared, looking very exhausted, and he stood before King Obatala.

The young man said, "I have handed over my wealth and the welfare of my sister to my uncle, and I am back to receive the penalty. You may execute it now."

Surprised, Obatala asked, "Why did you return after having a chance to escape the death penalty?"

The young man calmly replied, "I was afraid it would appear that humanity has lost its integrity and the ability to fulfil promises made."

Obatala turned to look at Lamurudu and asked him, "And why did you stand for him?"

Lamurudu responded, "I was afraid it might appear that humanity has lost the will to do good to others."

These words and events moved the complainant brothers, who had wanted justice for their father's death very deeply, and they decided to forgive the young goat herdsman.

When Obatala questioned them on their decision, they said, "We are afraid it will appear as though forgiveness has lost its place in the heart of humanity."

It is our duty to keep humanity and its essence alive.

21. Best Friend

Once, in a town bus packed to capacity, a small boy stood among a crowd of adults, holding onto a scrap of wood carefully. He was having a tough time ensuring that the jostling crowd of passengers did not knock the scrap out of his hand.

A lady who had been observing him for some time couldn't bear the suspense any longer.

"Why are you holding onto that little scrap so carefully?" she asked him, raising her voice above the roar of the engine.

He turned to her and replied earnestly, "I'm taking Lucy for a ride. She's my friend, and this is her first trip on a bus."

"But...but where's Lucy?" the lady asked, bewildered.

"Look carefully," said the little boy, drawing her attention to the scrap of wood. "Lucy is a little ant. I found her in my garden, and she is now my best friend!"

How imaginative, kind, sweet, and innocent!

Little deeds of kindness, little words of love, make our Earth an Eden, like the heaven above.

22. Coffee on the Wall

One evening, Samarth was in a well-known coffee shop with his friend in a neighbouring town of Venice, Italy, also known as the city of lights and water.

As they were enjoying their coffee, an old man entered and sat at an empty table next to them. He called the waiter and placed his order, saying, "Two cups of coffee, one on the wall."

Samarth and his friend noticed that the man was served one cup but paid for two. When he left, the waiter placed a cup on the wall with a note saying, 'A Cup of Coffee'.

While they were still there, two men came in and ordered three cups of coffee. They drank two but paid for three and left. This time again, the waiter placed a cup on the wall with a note saying, 'A Cup of Coffee'.

This seemed unique and perplexing to Samarth and his friend. They were getting late, so they finished, paid the bill, and left.

After a few days, Samarth visited the shop again. While he was having his coffee, a shabbily dressed man entered. He sat down, looked at the wall, and said, "One cup from the wall."

The waiter offered him the coffee with customary respect and dignity. The man enjoyed it and left without paying.

Samarth watched, stunned, as the waiter took off a piece of paper from the wall and threw it in the trash bin. Now, the matter was very clear to Samarth.

Tears welled up in Samarth's eyes at the respect shown to needy people like that man. He recollected how the poor man entered the shop with dignity, how he did not have to ask for a free cup, and how he was served the same coffee as everyone else without asking or knowing about the one who had paid for it. He only had to look at the wall, place an order for himself, and enjoy his coffee.

Samarth asked himself, "Can we help somebody and also ensure their dignity is maintained?"

Can we help somebody and also ensure that they keep their dignity intact in the process?

23. The Poor Eyesight

Siddharth was in Sydney Harbour, gazing at the beautiful bridge that joined the two halves of the city, when an Australian came up to him and requested him to read out an advertisement in the newspaper. "The print is too small," he said. "I can't make out what it says."

Siddharth tried but failed, as he didn't have his reading glasses with him. He apologized to the man.

"Oh, that's all right," the man said. Then he continued, "Do you know something? I think that God suffers from poor eyesight too, not because He's old, but because that's how He wants it to be. That way, when someone does something wrong, He can always say He couldn't quite see and so ends up forgiving the person because He doesn't want to commit an injustice."

"And what if someone does something good?" Siddharth asked.

"Ah, well," laughed the Australian, moving off. "God, of course, never leaves his glasses at home!"

Choose kindness over everything else!

24. The Last Cab Ride

Benny was a cab driver, and he narrated his most memorable experience at a gathering. He said, "Twenty years ago, I drove a cab for a living. One time, I arrived in the middle of the night for a pick-up at a building that was dark except for a single light in a ground-floor window. Under such circumstances, many drivers would just honk once or twice, wait a minute, and then drive away. However, I had seen too many impoverished people who depended on taxis as their only means of transportation. Unless a situation smelled of danger, I always went to the door. This passenger might be someone who needs my assistance, I reasoned to myself. So I walked to the door and knocked. 'Just a minute,' answered a frail, elderly voice.

"I could hear something being dragged across the floor. After a long pause, the door opened. A small woman in her 80s stood before me. She was wearing a printed dress and a pillbox hat with a veil pinned on it, like somebody out of a 1940s movie. By her side was a small nylon suitcase. The apartment looked as if no one had lived in it for years. All the furniture was covered with sheets. There were no clocks on the walls, no knick-knacks or utensils on the counters. In the corner was a cardboard box filled with photos and glassware.

"'Would you carry my bag out to the car?' she asked. I took the suitcase to the cab, then returned to assist the woman. She took my arm, and we walked slowly towards the cab. She kept thanking me for my kindness.

"It's nothing,' I told her. 'I just try to treat my passengers the way I would want my mother treated.'

"'Oh, you're such a good boy,' she said.

"When we got in the cab, she gave me an address, then asked, 'Could you drive through downtown?'

"'It's not the shortest way,' I answered quickly.

"'Oh, I don't mind,' she said. 'I'm in no hurry. I'm on my way to a hospice.' I looked at her in the rear-view mirror. Her eyes were glistening. 'I don't have any family left,' she continued. 'The doctor says I don't have very long to live.'

"I quietly reached over and shut off the metre. 'What route would you like me to take?' I asked.

"For the next two hours, we drove through the city. She showed me the building where she had once worked as an elevator operator. We drove through the neighbourhood where she and her husband had lived when they were newlyweds. She had me pull up in front of a furniture warehouse that had once been a ballroom where she had gone dancing as a girl. Sometimes she'd ask me to slow down in front of a particular building or corner and would sit staring into the darkness, saying nothing.

"As the first hint of sunlight was creasing the horizon, she suddenly said, 'I'm tired. Let's go now.'

"We drove in silence to the address she had given me. It was a low building, like a small convalescent home, with a driveway that passed under a portico. Two orderlies came out to the cab as soon as we pulled up. They were solicitous and intent, watching her every move. They must have been expecting her. I opened the trunk and took the small suitcase to the door. The woman was already seated in a wheelchair. 'How much do I owe you?' she asked, reaching into her purse.

"'Nothing,' I said.

"'You have to make a living,' she answered.

"'There are other passengers.' Almost without thinking, I bent down and gave her a hug.

"She held onto me tightly. 'You gave an old woman a little moment of joy,' she said. 'Thank you.'

"I squeezed her hand, then walked into the dim morning light. Behind me, a door shut. It was the sound of the closing of a life.

"I didn't pick up any more passengers that shift. I drove aimlessly, lost in thought. For the rest of that day, I could hardly talk. What if that woman had got an angry driver or one who was impatient to end his shift? What if I had refused to take the run or had honked once, then driven away? On a quick review, I don't think I have done anything more important in my life.

"We're conditioned to think that our lives revolve around great moments. But great moments often catch us unaware, beautifully wrapped in what others may consider a small one."

Sometimes we don't realize what a little gesture could mean to somebody else.

ACTION TIME

1. How do you feel about the stories?
2. What are your learnings?
3. What things will you do differently from now on and how?

(Please refer to the stories if needed.)

Little things you can try:

- Do a chore for someone silently without letting them know, and observe how you feel seeing them happy.
- Let someone go ahead of you in line.
- Call your grandparents/parents and let them know that you miss them and treasure them.

SELF-WORTH

Your value doesn't decrease based on someone's inability to see your worth.
You are not the labels you receive.
The world begins labelling you right from day one, but it's your duty to remember that these labels serve the world's convenience, not your potential.

1. Write down how the following people describe you:
   - Your parents
   - Your friends
   - Your partner
   - Your bosses or teachers

Which of these descriptions do you identify with the most? Which of these tags have you been conforming to all along?

2. Are you really defined solely by the degrees you hold, the pay package you earn, the number of followers you have on social media, or the number of likes you receive on your posts? Is that your true worth?

25. Knowledge Does Matter

A man found an eagle's egg and put it in the nest of a backyard hen. The eaglet hatched with the brood of chicks and grew up with them.

In the beginning, he felt a little different from the chickens; he thought he looked bigger. However, everyone around him kept telling him that he was just another chicken. After a while, he began to believe he was one.

He would do what the backyard chickens did. He would scratch the earth for worms and insects, cluck and cackle, and thrash his wings and fly a few feet into the air.

Years passed, and the eagle grew very old. One day, he saw a magnificent bird far above him in the cloudless sky. The majestic bird glided gracefully among the powerful wind currents, with scarcely a beat of its strong golden wings. The old eagle was awestruck and asked, "Who's that?"

"That's the eagle, the king of the birds," replied a chicken. "He belongs to the sky, while we belong to the earth—we're chickens."

The eagle caught a glimpse of his reflection in a nearby pond. He had a moment of clarity and realized that he was not a chicken, but an eagle, a lord of the skies.

But had that knowledge come too late?

He climbed up a tree, spread his wings, and jumped. Sure enough, the eagle in him took over, and he soared across the skies.

Just because he was told he was a chicken, he began to believe he was one. This holds true for us as well. It's time we realize who we truly are rather than conforming to what the world tells us!

It's hard to be yourself in a world where everyone is trying to make you be somebody else.

26. You are the Light

Once, there was a talented and vibrant young boy, but as he entered his teenage years, he became too lazy. He would waste his time sleeping or watching TV and never put his talents to any use. This was a serious concern for his family.

One day, his uncle paid him a visit. Late at night, there was a power cut. The boy noticed his uncle doing something strange—he lit two candles and placed one under a bowl and the other behind a chair.

The young boy laughed. "Uncle, how strange! Why are you placing the candles so? Of what use are they, now that their light has been hidden?"

His uncle smiled and replied, "Just as it is with these candles, so it is with us. Talent, when hidden or not put to any good use, is of no benefit to anyone. Do not be a candle whose light is hidden; be a candle whose light shines out, dispelling darkness."

The boy understood the wisdom of his uncle's words.

Remember, your light can brighten the world! Let's illuminate it!

27. How to Take Feedback

An aspiring artist had just completed his training under one of the finest painters in the world. Full of enthusiasm, he painstakingly painted a beautiful landscape. On completing the painting, he wanted feedback on it. So, he displayed it at a busy street crossing, and near it, he placed a small sign that read:

'I have painted this piece. Since I'm new to this profession, I may have committed a few mistakes. Please put a cross wherever you see a mistake.'

When he returned in the evening to collect his painting, he was completely shattered to see the whole canvas filled with crosses. Some people had even written their comments on the painting.

Disheartened, he went to his teacher. "Sir, people have rejected my work completely," he said despondently. "My first painting ever is filled with mistakes. I don't feel I have done justice to your teaching. I don't believe I am a good artist."

The teacher smiled and said, "Son, don't be discouraged by negative feedback. I will prove to you that you are a great artist and that your painting is perfectly executed. Just do what I say, and you will see."

The young artist agreed, and two days later, he presented a replica of his earlier painting to his teacher.

"Come with me," said the teacher.

They reached the same street square early in the morning and displayed the replica at the same place. The teacher put up a sign that read: 'I have painted this piece. Since I'm new to this profession, I may have committed a few mistakes. I have kept colours and brushes just below. If you see a mistake, please be so kind as to pick up a brush and correct it.'

When the young painter visited the spot later in the evening, he was surprised to see that not even a single correction had been made. He left the painting at the square for a month, but no corrections were ever made!

The painter asked his teacher why no corrections were made in the second painting, even though both paintings were the same. The teacher replied smilingly, "It is easy to pass judgement and criticize what is being done, but it is difficult to improve it."

Believe in yourself and your abilities. Don't judge yourself based on unwarranted criticism.

28. Where to Strike

Once, a ship was stranded at a small port in a foreign country. The engineer in charge of the ship could not repair the engine, which had stopped suddenly. The captain of the ship inquired from the local inhabitants if there was any engineer nearby who could repair the engine.

He was informed that a retired marine engineer was settled in a small village in the vicinity. The captain contacted him and requested that he repair the engine of the ship. The engineer came and inspected the engine. He struck a hammer gently in a few places, and the engine started working.

When the captain asked the engineer about his charges, he replied that he be paid $10,000. The captain was shocked and retorted, "You are charging $10,000 just for striking a hammer?"

The marine engineer then asked the captain how much he should have charged, to which the latter replied that the maximum should have been $500.

The marine engineer quickly replied, "I am charging $500 for 'just striking the hammer' and the balance of $9500 for 'knowing where to strike the hammer'."

Know Your Worth!

29. I am Stupid

Once, as a prank, a classmate stuck a paper on a student's back that read: 'I'm stupid'. He asked the rest of the class not to tell the boy. This joke among the classmates remained a secret from the student throughout the day. As the day proceeded towards the last period, the mathematics class began, and the teacher wrote a question on the board.

The question was difficult, and no one was able to answer it except the boy with the sticker. Amidst snickering, he walked towards the board and solved the question. The teacher asked the class to clap for him and removed the paper that was stuck on his back.

The teacher said, "You don't know that one of your classmates stuck a paper on your back, and the rest of them kept it a secret."

Then the teacher turned to the class and said, "Let me tell you something: Throughout your life, people will put labels on your back with bad things written on them to hinder your progress. If this boy had known about the paper, he would not have stood up to answer the question. Similarly, all you have to do in life is ignore the labels people give you, and use every chance you have to progress, learn, and improve yourself."

To the person placing the label, it's just an innocuous remark or tag, but it may cause a lifetime's worth of damage to the person receiving it. Placing tags on people, sometimes unintentionally, can harm them beyond imagination.

We always have an opportunity to tag or praise people. Praising someone daily is a healthy habit.

30. Identify Your Fit

A mother camel and her baby were lying down, soaking up the sun. The baby camel asked his mother, "Why do we have these big bumps on our back?"

The mother camel took a moment to think and then replied, "We live in the desert where not much water is available. Our humps help us survive long journeys."

The baby camel thought for a while and then asked, "Why do we have long legs with rounded feet?"

His mother replied, "They help us walk through sand."

The baby asked a third question, "Why are my eyelashes so long?"

The mother answered, "Your long eyelashes offer you protection from sand when it blows with the wind."

Finally, the baby said, "If all of these natural abilities have been given to us to walk through the desert, what's their use for camels in the zoo?"

The mother camel could not answer this question.

The skills and abilities that you possess won't be useful if you're not in the right environment. You've probably heard of a professional who ditched their career to follow their dreams or a person who remains unfulfilled in their job but doesn't try to make a change.

If you're stuck in a situation, identify your right fit, make the required move, and reach a place where you fit in the best.

Don't be a camel stuck in a zoo.

31. Who Would Like this Twenty-Dollar Bill?

Once there was a lecturer who began a seminar by holding up a twenty-dollar bill and asking, "Who would like this twenty-dollar bill?" Several hands went up, but the lecturer said, "Before I give it to you, I have to do something." He crumpled it up into a ball and asked, "Who still wants this bill?" The hands went up again. Then he asked, "And what if I do this to it?" He threw the crumpled bill at the wall. It fell on the floor, after which he insulted it, trampled on it, and once more showed it to them, now all creased and dirty. He repeated the question, and the hands stayed up. "Never forget this scene," he said. "It doesn't matter what I do with this money; it is still a twenty-dollar bill. Often in our lives, we are crumpled, trampled, ill-treated, and insulted. Yet, despite all that, we are still worth the same."

Your worth isn't dependent on external factors but on what lies within you.

32. A Label

Nitin sat in his chair quietly next to his parents as his Grade 4 teacher, Mrs Shastri, gave them an update on his progress at school.

"Nitin is a slow learner," said Mrs Shastri quietly.

Nitin held his breath and sank a little lower into his chair. He looked up at his father, fearing he was in trouble. His father glanced down at him, smiled, and gave him a quick wink. On the way home from the Parent-Teacher meeting, Nitin thought about what Mrs Shastri had called him—'slow learner'. Deep down, he knew what she really meant was that he was dumb.

Later that evening, his parents came into his room, carrying a piece of paper and a pen. They sat down on the bed and said, "We want to talk to you about what Mrs Shastri said today."

"A 'slow learner'," he replied. He had taken the words to heart.

"That's right," said his father as his mother wrote the words 'slow learner' on the piece of paper. His mother then held up the paper in front of him and tore it into two.

Nitin's eyes widened in surprise.

"Mrs Shastri was wrong," said his mother as she continued to tear the paper into smaller pieces. "You're not a slow learner."

"I'm not?" asked Nitin.

"No, and starting tomorrow, you and I are going to prove Mrs Shastri was wrong, OK?" his father replied.

"OK." Nitin hugged his parents, snuggled down into his pillow, and fell asleep with a smile on his face and a warm glow in his heart.

From that day on, his parents spent one hour every day helping him with his reading and writing. By the end of the year, he was doing much better at school, and no one ever labelled him a 'slow learner' again.

You are not the labels you receive.

ACTION TIME

1. How do you feel about the stories?
2. What are your learnings?
3. What things will you do differently from now on and how?

(Please refer to the stories if needed.)

Prepare a list of the roles you play and another one of all the labels people gave you.

Write a letter to yourself, expressing deep appreciation, recognition, and acceptance. Include your struggles, victories, failures, successes, moments of loss, and how wonderfully you have evolved throughout the journey.

THE LIFE BATTLES

Choose your battles.
Not every race is worth running,
not every challenge is worth accepting.
Be a good person, but don't waste your time proving it.

1. Observe the image given below:

Why do you think the cheetah didn't feel the need to run this race and refused to even step out?

2. Is it necessary to justify one's actions or explain oneself to everyone? Is every battle worth the fight?

33. Why Carry Rotten Potatoes?

Once, a junior school teacher asked her students to bring some potatoes in a plastic bag to school. She explained, "Each potato will be given the name of the person whom that child hates. In this way, the number of potatoes each child has will be equal to the number of people they hate."

On the decided day, the children brought their potatoes with the names of the people they hated written on them. Some had two, some had three, and some even had five potatoes.

The teacher instructed that they would have to carry these potatoes with them everywhere they go for a week.

As the days passed, the children began to complain about the stale smell emanating from these potatoes. Additionally, some students who had many potatoes complained that they were very heavy to carry around. The assignment was over after a week, and the children were relieved.

The teacher asked, "How did you feel during this one week?"

The children mentioned their problems with the smell and weight.

Then the teacher said, "This situation is very similar to what happens when you carry hatred in your heart for some people. The hatred makes your heart unhealthy, and you carry that hatred everywhere you go. If you can't bear the smell of spoiled potatoes for a week, imagine the impact on your heart of this hatred that you carry throughout your life."

Our heart is a beautiful garden that needs regular cleaning of unwanted weeds. Forgive those who have not behaved with you as expected, and forget the bad things. This also makes room for storing good things.

Your heart is precious. Choose wisely what you burden it with.

34. The Story of the Donkey and the Tiger

The donkey said to the tiger, "The grass is blue."

The tiger retorted, "No, the grass is green."

The discussion became heated, and the two decided to take the issue before the lion, the king of the jungle.

When they reached the clearing in the forest where the lion was sitting on his throne, the donkey asked, "Your Highness, is it true that the grass is blue?"

The lion replied, "Yes, the grass is blue."

The donkey rushed forward and continued, "The tiger disagrees with me and annoys me. Please punish him."

The king then declared, "The tiger will be punished with five years of silence."

The donkey jumped with joy and went on his way, content and repeating, "The grass is blue! The grass is blue!"

The tiger asked the lion, "Your Majesty, why have you punished me? After all, the grass is green."

The lion replied, "Yes, the grass is green."

The tiger asked, "So why did you punish me?"

The lion replied, "That has nothing to do with the question of whether the grass is blue or green. I have punished you because a brave and intelligent creature like you not only has wasted time arguing with a donkey but also has come and bothered me with that question."

The worst waste of time is arguing with a fool and a fanatic who doesn't care about truth or reality but only the victory of their beliefs and illusions. Never waste time on discussions that make no sense.

There are people who, for all the evidence presented to them, do not have the ability to understand. There are others who are blinded by ego, hatred, and resentment, and the only thing they want is to be right, even if they aren't.

When ignorance screams, intelligence shuts up. Your peace and tranquillity are worth more.

35. Race

No one has ever bothered to ask the hare his side of the story, so let me tell you what he wants to tell the world.

The hare was asked to sit down for a heart-to-heart talk, and this is what he had to say:

Yes, I am the hare who lost. No, I did not get lazy or complacent. Let me explain what happened.

I was hopping over the meadows near the hills and looked back to realize that the tortoise was nowhere to be seen. Assured of my healthy lead, I decided to take a short nap under a large banyan tree near the pond.

The anticipation of the race had kept me up all night. For days, that silly old tortoise had boasted about his ability to plod on for hundreds of miles without stopping. Life is a marathon, he said, not a sprint. I wanted to show him that I could run both far and fast.

It was cool in the shade of the tree. I found an almost oval rock, covered it with grass, and turned it into a makeshift pillow. I could hear the leaves rustling and the bees buzzing, as if collaborating and even conspiring to put me to sleep. It didn't take them long to succeed.

I dreamt of myself drifting on a log in a beautiful stream. As I neared the shore, I saw an old man with a flowing beard sitting on a rock in a meditative pose. He opened his eyes and smiled at me knowingly.

He asked, "Who are you?"

"I am a hare. I am running a race."

"Why?"

"To prove to all the creatures in the jungle that I am the fastest."

"Why do you want to prove that you are the fastest?"

"So that I get a medal, which will give me status, which will give me money, which will get me food."

"There is already so much food around." He pointed to the forest in the distance. "Look at all those trees laden with fruits and nuts, as well as those leafy branches."

"I also want respect. I want to be remembered as the fastest hare who ever lived."

"Do you know the name of the fastest deer, the largest elephant, or the strongest lion that lived a thousand years before you?"

"No."

"Today, you have been challenged by a tortoise. Tomorrow, it will be a snake. Then it will be a zebra. Will you keep racing all your life to prove that you are the fastest?"

"Hmm. I didn't think about it. I don't want to race all my life."

"What do you want to do?"

"I want to sleep under a banyan tree on a makeshift pillow while the leaves rustle and the bees buzz. I want to hop over the meadows near the hills and swim in the pond."

"You can do all these things at this very moment. Forget the race. You are here today, but you will be gone tomorrow."

I woke up from my sleep. The ducks in the pond looked happy. I jumped in, startling them for a moment. They looked at me quizzically. "Weren't you supposed to be racing with the tortoise today?"

"It's pointless, an exercise in futility. All I want is to be here."

Hopefully, someday, someone will tell the world my story—I lost the race but got my life back.

Live life to the fullest, today, tomorrow, and always.

36. Unnecessary Burdens

One day, two monks were walking through the countryside. They were on their way to another village to help bring in the crops. As they walked, they found a sad old woman sitting at the edge of a river. She was upset because there was no bridge, and she could not get across on her own.

The first monk kindly offered, "We will carry you across if you would like."

"Thank you," she said gratefully, accepting their help. So the two men joined hands, lifted her between them, and carried her across the river. When they got to the other side, they set her down, and she went her way.

After they had walked another mile or so, the second monk began to complain. "Look at my clothes," he said. "They are filthy from carrying that woman across the river. And my back still hurts from lifting her. I can feel it getting stiff." The first monk just smiled and nodded.

A few more miles up the road, the second monk grumbled again, "My back is hurting badly, and it is all because we had to carry that silly woman across the river. I cannot go any further because of the pain."

The first monk looked down at his partner, now lying on the ground, moaning. "Have you wondered why I am not complaining?" he asked. "Your back hurts because you are still carrying the woman, but I set her down five miles ago."

This is how many of us deal with our lives. We are the second monk who cannot let go. We hold the pain of the past over our loved ones' heads like a club, or we remind them every once in a while, when we want to get the upper hand, of the burden we still carry because of something they did years ago.

Get rid of all bitterness, rage and anger, brawling and slander, along with every form of hatred and feel lighter by letting go of unnecessary burdens.

Check if you are still carrying something you should have left behind way back.

37. The Elephant and the Pig

An elephant was travelling along its route after bathing in a river. As it approached a bridge, it noticed a pig walking towards it, completely covered in dirty mud.

The elephant calmly moved to one side, allowing the filthy pig to pass, and then proceeded on its way.

"See how big and important I am; even the elephant was terrified of me and stepped aside to allow me to pass," the dirty pig later boasted to its friends.

When word got around and the elephant's friends heard of this incident, several of them asked their friend, "Was it really due to fear that you moved to the side?"

"I could have easily crushed the pig beneath my foot," the elephant replied, "but I was clean, and the pig was quite dirty. Moreover, crushing it would have made my leg muddy, something I wanted to avoid. Hence, I stepped aside."

A wise person will avoid contact with negativity, not out of fear but due to the preference to avoid impurity, even if they are powerful enough to eliminate it. We do not need to react to every opposing viewpoint, word, or scenario.

Not every situation deserves your reaction.

38. Charity Under Threat

Once, Albert and his wife went to the aid of a Swiss tourist in Ipanema, who claimed he had been robbed by some street children. Speaking appalling Portuguese in a thick foreign accent, he said that he had been left without his passport, without any money, and with nowhere to sleep. Albert's wife, being compassionate, bought him lunch, gave him enough cash to pay for a hotel room for the night while he got in touch with his embassy, and then left. Days later, a Rio newspaper reported that this 'Swiss tourist' was, in fact, an inventive con artist who faked an accent and abused the good faith of those who love Rio. When she read the article, Albert's wife simply said, "Well, that's not going to stop me from helping anyone."

Her remark reminded Albert of the story of a wise man who moved to the city of Akbar. No one took much notice of him, and his teachings were not popular among the populace. After a while, he became the object of their mockery and ironic comments. One day, while he was walking down the main street, a group of men and women began insulting him. Instead of ignoring them, the wise man turned and blessed them. One of the men asked, "Are you deaf, too? We call you the foulest of names, and yet you respond with sweet words!"

"Each of us can only offer what we have," replied the wise man.

Let's be who we are, irrespective of what we can be.

39. The One Bad Apple

Once upon a time, there lived an apple farmer. He was very good at growing apples, and it gave him great satisfaction to see his hard work over the year come to fruition with a glorious harvest.

On one particular morning, as the farmer was taking his dog for a walk, he noticed something odd.

One bad apple was sitting high up on his most prized bountiful tree. "If that one bad apple were to spoil the rest of the apples and then the rest of the field, my whole crop would be damaged," he said to himself. "I must do something, but what?"

He went to the tractor shed to fetch a long pole. "This way, I can poke it out of the tree and stop the problem from spreading," he thought. However, try as he might, the pole just wasn't long enough, and in the attempt to get that one bad apple, a few good ones were knocked to the ground.

"This is no good," he said to himself. "I need a better idea." He returned to the tractor shed, this time for a catapult. "I can shoot the one bad apple off its branch, and my problem will be solved," he thought.

Despite trying hard, the farmer couldn't hit that one bad apple as his aim wasn't very good. In all the badly aimed and missed attempts, a few good apples were again knocked to the ground.

"This is also no good," he thought. "I need a better solution—one that is foolproof." This time, his plan was to shake the tree so that the one bad apple might fall to the ground, solving the problem once and for all.

However, no matter how hard the farmer shook the tree, that

one bad apple just wouldn't budge. In all his attempts, a few good apples were shaken loose and fell to the ground.

A few more days passed, and the farmer was now obsessed with that one bad apple sitting at the top of the tree. With one final foolproof plan of attack in his mind, the farmer armed himself with a chainsaw. He had decided that if he couldn't poke, shoot, or shake it out of the tree, then he was going to cut off the branch. That way, he was certain to rid himself of that one bad apple.

The farmer arrived at his prized apple tree and noticed something for the first time. With all his concentration and days being taken up with that one bad apple, he had knocked, shaken, and poked all the other apples to the ground, where they lay rotting. In an attempt to stop the rot of that one bad apple spreading to the rest, he had failed to notice all the other wonderful apples that had ripened on his prized apple tree.

Sometimes, we spend too much time and effort looking at the one bad apple in our lives. What we forget to do is remember all the other wonderful apples we already have sitting on our apple tree.

Remember to not forget your several blessings just because of that one problem.

ACTION TIME

1. How do you feel about the stories?
2. What are your learnings?
3. What things will you do differently from now on and how?

(Please refer to the stories if needed.)

Know the 5-minute-5-year rule! Each time there is something that bothers you, ask yourself: Will this matter or make a difference 5 years from now? If not, don't spend more than 5 minutes worrying or stressing about it. Your time is precious.

List some of the pressing issues that concern you at present and then analyze them as per the 5-minute-5-year rule.

What is your biggest fear and why?

PERSEVERANCE

Obstacles are opportunities in disguise.
Every rock on the path is not meant to be a blockade; at times, it's just the Almighty helping you collect the stones you need for building your dream fort. What's important is that you persevere and keep moving.
Remember, the best view comes after the hardest climb!

1. J. K. Rowling, author of the Harry Potter series of books, was rejected by every publishing house she approached, and the rest is history! Read about her inspirational journey.
2. How many times have you felt grateful in hindsight for a challenge that seemed a nightmare when you were facing it?

40. Rock on the Path

A king once ordered a boulder to be placed on a road. He then hid and waited to see if anyone would care to move the massive rock aside. Some of the richest merchants and courtiers of the king passed by and simply strolled past it. Some even criticized the king for failing to maintain the roads, but nobody tried to move the stone.

A peasant then arrived, hauling a load of vegetables. He walked up to the boulder, dropped his load, and tried to roll the stone to the side of the path. He struggled and pushed hard before succeeding.

When the peasant went back to pick up his load of vegetables, he noticed a purse lying on the road where the boulder had been. The purse contained several gold coins and a note from the king indicating that the gold was for the person who removed the boulder from the roadway.

The peasant learned what many of us never understand…

Every obstacle presents an opportunity for growth and progress.

41. The Hope Experiment

During a brutal study at Harvard in the 1950s, Dr Curt Richter placed rats in a pool of water to test how long they could tread water.

On average, they'd give up and begin to sink after 15 minutes.

But right before they gave up due to exhaustion, the researchers would pluck them out, dry them off, let them rest for a few minutes, and then put them back in for a second round.

They had swum until exhaustion only a few minutes ago, so how long do you think they lasted in this second round?

Another 15 minutes? 10 minutes? 5 minutes? No!

60 hours! That's right! 60 hours of swimming!

The conclusion drawn was that since the rats believed they would eventually be rescued, they could push their bodies beyond what they previously thought impossible.

We will leave you with this thought:

If hope can cause exhausted rats to swim for that long, what could belief in yourself and your abilities do for you?

These are testing times, but believe that everything will be fine.

Keep hope and keep fighting.

42. It Becomes Easier

Once upon a time, a wealthy king sought a suitable man to marry his daughter. He decided to create a challenge to test whether an individual had the appropriate attitude and would not quit at the first indication of adversity. To pass the test, each candidate had to don the royal metallic armour and climb 1000 stairs to the top of the mountain, where the king's palace was located.

Many men gathered from across the world to take on the task. However, as soon as they put on the armour, they understood that the endeavour would be impossible.

The majority of men climbed the first step, then glanced up at the remaining 999 and gave up. Several made it to the second step before abandoning their quest. And so it continued for the next couple of hundred men, with some reaching the third step. Many who came to try their luck stayed away after seeing others who attempted to compete in the challenge and failed miserably. The king was worried. He pondered if anyone was deserving of his daughter.

So far, everyone had failed, and they were discussing how the task was designed to be impossible to finish. The most powerful military men, top athletes, and even the most muscular men attempted and failed. They all blamed the armour and the steps. If only the armour were lighter, if only the stairs weren't so steep...

Then, to everyone's astonishment, a young man, who appeared to be very ordinary and not very impressive, declared he wanted to try. He, like everyone else before him, had his chance. He donned the heavy gear and proceeded to the steps. Everyone predicted he wouldn't make it past the first step, but he was quick to reach the second and then the third.

Although he could hardly move his shivering feet to the fourth step, he took a deep breath and pressed forward. He felt on the verge of collapse, but he was determined to keep going. He kept telling himself, "One step at a time. I only have to finish this one." As he approached the fifth step, he felt a strong pull from the top. His armour became noticeably lighter. So he took another step, telling himself, "I'm not ready to quit yet."

Surprisingly, the armour felt even lighter at this stage. He was exhausted but determined to take one more step. So the 'not-so-special young man' went on. Each stride made his armour lighter and brought his goal closer.

When the young man finished the challenge, the king praised him and then revealed a secret about the test: "The challenge aimed to ensure that the person who marries my daughter is not the type of man who gives up after the first couple of difficult moments."

Maybe it's about just one more step, just one more time of getting up, just one more try. Don't give up!

ACTION TIME

1. How do you feel about the stories?
2. What are your learnings?
3. What things will you do differently from now on and how?

(Please refer to the stories if needed.)

Sometimes, just when you are about to give up, all you need to do is try one more time to accomplish what you want. You must have experiences where you thought of giving up, and then something made you persevere, and you succeeded! Recollect some of those experiences and remind yourself of the magic of perseverance.

List your quarterly goals or three important tasks that you will accomplish today.

Pick one important task that has been pending for days and complete it today.

MAKING A DIFFERENCE

Even the tiniest bit matters! Maybe not today but tomorrow, maybe not to you but to someone else, but it does make a difference!

"If you think you are too small to make a difference...try sleeping with a mosquito in the room." – Dalai Lama.

1. The amount of food we, at times, leave on our plates is all that a family has in an entire day. Many small things that we tend to overlook can be of immense significance to someone else. Give it a thought.
2. Do you carry your cloth/jute/paper bag every time you go out shopping? If others don't, will you doing it alone make any difference?

43. It Makes a Difference

One morning, a man was taking a walk at the beach. He noticed that along with the morning tide came hundreds of starfish, but when the tide receded, they were left behind and would die from being exposed to the morning sun rays. The man took a few steps, picked one up, and threw it into the water. He did so repeatedly. Behind him was another person who couldn't understand what this man was doing. He caught up with him and asked, "What are you doing? There are hundreds of starfish. How many can you save? What difference does it make?"

The man took two more steps, picked up another one, threw it into the water, and replied, "It makes a difference to this one."

If it makes a difference to even one, it's worth it.

44. Does it Matter to You?

A man was walking past a construction site when he saw a sculptor chiselling a statue of an idol. He noticed an identical statue lying nearby in the corner.

Curious, the man asked the sculptor, "Do you need two statues of the same idol?"

"No," said the sculptor without looking up. "We need only one, but the first one got damaged at the last stage."

The man examined the discarded statue carefully. There seemed to be no apparent damage. "The idol seems to be perfectly fine to me," he said.

"Well, look carefully," said the sculptor, still busy with his work. "There is a scratch on the nose of the idol."

"Where are you going to install the idol?" asked the man.

The sculptor replied that it would be installed on a pillar 20 feet high.

"If the statue is to be placed so far away, no one would be able to see the scratch on the idol's nose. It is such a tiny flaw; it doesn't matter," the man said.

The sculptor stopped his work, looked up at the man, smiled, and said, "It matters to me."

Perfection and excellence come from surpassing the benchmarks we set for ourselves.

45. Be Someone's Light

Some years ago, a bus full of passengers was stuck on a cross-town route in New York City during rush hour. Traffic was barely moving. The bus was filled with cold, tired people who were deeply irritated with one another and the world itself.

Two men barked at each other about a shove that might or might not have been intentional. A pregnant woman boarded the bus, but nobody offered her a seat. Rage was in the air; no mercy would be found there.

However, as the bus approached Seventh Avenue, the driver's voice came over the intercom. "Folks," he said, "I know you have had a rough day and are frustrated. I can't do anything about the weather or traffic, but here is what I can do. As each one of you gets off the bus, I will reach out my hand to you. As you walk by, drop your troubles into the palm of my hand, okay? Don't take your problems home to your families tonight, just leave them with me. My route goes right by the Hudson River, and when I drive by there later, I will open the window and throw your troubles in the water."

It was as if a spell had lifted. Everyone burst out laughing. Faces gleamed with surprised delight. People who had been pretending for the past hour not to notice each other's existence were suddenly grinning at each other.

At the next stop, just as promised, the driver reached out his hand, palm up, and waited. One by one, all the exiting commuters placed their hand just above his and mimed the gesture of dropping something into his palm. Some people laughed as they did this, others teared up, but everyone did it. The driver repeated the same lovely ritual at the next stop, too. And the next. All the way to the river.

We live in a hard world, where sometimes it is extremely difficult to be a human being. Sometimes you have a bad day. Sometimes you have a bad day that lasts for several years. You struggle and fail. You lose jobs, money, friends, faith, and love. You witness horrible events unfolding in the news, and you become fearful and withdrawn. There are times when everything seems cloaked in darkness. You long for the light but don't know where to find it.

This bus driver taught everyone that anyone can be the light, at any moment. He wasn't some big power player. He wasn't a spiritual leader. He wasn't some media-savvy influencer. He was a bus driver, one of society's most invisible workers. But he possessed real power, and he used it beautifully for the benefit of others. When life feels especially grim, or when you feel particularly powerless in the face of the world's troubles, think of this man and ask yourself, "What can I do, right now, to be the light?" Of course, you can't personally end all wars, prevent global warming, control traffic, or transform vexatious people into entirely different creatures. But you do have some influence on everyone you come in contact with, even if you never speak or learn each other's names. No matter who you are, where you are, or how mundane or tough your situation may seem, believe you can illuminate the world.

In fact, this is the only way the world will ever be illuminated, one bright act of grace at a time, all the way to the river.

46. Create Miracles

A certain company had a tradition of hosting a party and holding a lottery draw every Christmas Eve. The rules of the lottery draw were as follows: Each employee paid ten dollars towards the fund. There being 300 people in the company, a total of three thousand dollars would be raised. One winner took all the money home.

On the day of the lottery draw, the atmosphere in the office was lively. Everyone wrote their names on slips of paper and put them in the lottery box.

However, a young man hesitated. He knew that the company's cleaning lady's frail and sickly son was to have an operation soon after the dawn of the new year, but she did not have enough money to pay for the operation, which made her quite troubled.

So, even though he knew that the chances of winning the lottery were slim—only 0.33 per cent—the man wrote the name of the cleaning lady on the note. The much-awaited moment finally arrived. The boss shoved his arm into the lottery box and drew out a note. The man kept praying in his heart, hoping against hope that the cleaning lady would win the prize. Then the boss announced the winner's name, and a miracle happened!

The winner turned out to be the cleaning lady. Cheers broke out in the office, and the cleaning lady rushed to the stage to accept the prize. She burst into tears and said, "I am so fortunate and blessed! With this money, my son now has hope!"

The party began. While thinking about this 'Christmas miracle', the man went up to the lottery box. He took out a folded piece of paper and opened it. The name on it was also that of the cleaning lady! The man was very surprised. He took out several pieces of paper, one after another.

Although the handwriting on them was different, all bore the name of the cleaning lady. The man's eyes filled with tears. He realized that there was such a thing as a Christmas miracle in the world, but the miracle did not fall from the sky—people were required to create it by themselves.

Your actions lead to miracles.

47. Let's Do Our Part

According to an old Native American legend, there was once a big fire in the forest, causing all the animals to flee in terror in all directions.

Suddenly, the jaguar saw a hummingbird fly over his head, but in the opposite direction, towards the fire!

Moments later, the jaguar saw it pass again, this time in the same direction as that of the jaguar. He observed this coming and going until he decided to ask the bird about its bizarre behaviour.

"What are you doing, hummingbird?" he asked.

"I am going to the lake," the bird answered. "I carry water in my beak and throw it on the fire to extinguish it."

The jaguar laughed. "Are you crazy? Do you really think you can put out that big fire on your own with your very small beak?"

"No," said the hummingbird. "I know I can't. But the forest is my home. It feeds me and shelters my family. I am very grateful for that, and I help the forest grow by pollinating its flowers. I am part of the forest, and the forest is part of me. I know I can't put out the fire, but I must do my part."

At that moment, the forest spirits, who had listened to the hummingbird, were moved by its devotion to the forest. Miraculously, they sent a torrential downpour, which put an end to the great fire.

Let's do our bit and hope for the miracle to transpire.

ACTION TIME

1. How do you feel about the stories?
2. What are your learnings?
3. What things will you do differently from now on and how?

(Please refer to the stories if needed.)

Try doing the following:

- Pick up trash/litter that you spot while walking across your home/office (even if it was thrown by someone else) and put it in the dustbin.
- Spend time with someone who needs to be heard without being judgemental.
- Donate to a cause or volunteer in a local social service drive.

THE BIG PICTURE

There is more than what meets the eye.
More often than we realize, we consider the partial to be the full. Our vision has its limitations, but our understanding and awareness can defy all such limits.
Remember to ask yourself: “Is it just what I see, or is there more that my eyes fail to observe?”

1. We all tend to make the mistake of believing the half-truth to be fact, when what meets the eye may just be the tip of the iceberg, don’t we?
2. Let’s play a quick game. List three adjectives that come to your mind when you hear the word ‘Africa’. Once you have written them down, refer to this video: https://youtu.be/D9Ihs241zeg
3. You will understand how important it is to try to look beyond what you can see!

48. We are also Blind

Once, a 24-year-old boy travelling on a train looked outside the window and shouted, "Dad, look, the trees are going behind!"

His father smiled, and a young couple sitting nearby looked at the boy with pity, thinking his behaviour was childish. Suddenly, he again exclaimed, "Dad, look, the clouds are running with us!"

The couple couldn't resist and asked the father, "Why don't you take your son to a good doctor?"

The old man smiled and replied, "I did. We are coming from the hospital. My son was blind from birth. He just started seeing today."

Every single person on the planet has a story.

Don't judge people before you truly know them. The truth might surprise you.

49. The Seasons of Life

There was once a man who had four young sons. Wanting to teach them about the dangers of judging things too quickly, he decided to send each of them on a journey, one after the other, to a distant pear tree. Each son went in a different season, the first in winter, the second in spring, and so on.

At the end of the year, the man brought his children together and asked them what they'd seen. The son who'd travelled in winter described a gnarled, twisted, and barren tree that stood stark and ugly against the land. The son who went in the spring disagreed. He recalled that the tree seemed full of hope and promise, with green buds along its branches. The third son, who'd travelled in summer, did not agree with either. The pear tree he had seen was covered in beautiful blossoms that looked and smelled divine. Finally, the last son, who'd made the journey in the fall, contradicted his three brothers, describing a tree laden with sweet and delicious pears that tasted better than any he'd eaten before.

When each son had spoken, the father said they were all correct because they'd only seen one season of the pear tree's life. He explained to his sons that it's foolish and impossible to judge anything in this manner. The essence of something, whether it's a tree or a fellow man, can only be measured as a whole, having observed it in its fullness.

To make your judgement in winter is to miss the promise of spring, the beauty of summer, and the fruit in fall. Refuse to judge yourself, life, or other people based upon a single mistake or challenging time.

Refuse to let the pain of one season destroy the joy of those to come.

50. Two Plus Two is Five

A teacher teaching maths to a class of six-year-olds asked a boy named Adi, "If I give you two mangoes and then another two, how many mangoes will you have?"

He answered, "Five."

She was surprised by his reply but tried again. This time, she used her fingers to make him count with her. "Ok, Adi, if I give you one, two, two mangoes and another one, two, two mangoes, how many mangoes will you have?"

He again answered, "Five."

This time, she was really annoyed by his answer, but she controlled her anger. She remembered his mother had once told her that he liked strawberries. So, she tried a new approach. "Ok, Adi, if I give you two strawberries and then another two, how many strawberries will you have?"

"Four," he replied.

She felt relieved that he was back on track. So, again she asked him, "Now tell me, Adi, if I give you two mangoes and then another two, how many mangoes will you have?"

He answered, "Teacher, five mangoes."

The teacher burst out in anger, "How can you have five mangoes if I give you only four?"

"Teacher, because I already have one mango in my bag." There was complete silence in the class for the next two minutes. The teacher calmed down but regretted losing her cool.

There are two sides to every story. We should not make a decision for others without knowing their point of view. We make a decision on the basis of the logical rightness, that is, the obvious answer, but we don't ever try to know the practical rightness, that is, the actual truth.

Know that there's always another side to the story.

51. Respect the 'NO'

Once, a bird was searching for a home to lay her eggs and take shelter in the rainy season. She saw two leafy trees and went to ask for protection.

When she asked the first tree, it refused to give her shelter. Disappointed, she approached the second tree, which agreed. She built her nest and laid her eggs. Then the rainy season arrived. It rained so heavily that the first tree fell and was carried away by the flood.

The bird saw this and taunted, "See, this is your karma. You didn't offer me shelter, and now God has punished you."

The fallen tree smiled for the last time and said, "I knew I was not going to survive this rainy season. That's why I refused to give you shelter. I didn't want to risk your and your children's lives."

The bird had tears in her eyes on hearing these words. The 'NO' that came her way was, in fact, a blessing.

Pause and think about an occurrence in life deeply before you judge it.

Sometimes you don't know that the rejection you just faced is in your best interest.

52. Sorry, I Didn't Hear You

There was once a watchman who used to open and close the gate of a house and then greet the house owner. However, the owner never responded. The watchman thought his owner was a little arrogant and didn't want to interact with someone of his stature.

Every day, after work, the watchman would search the garbage for food—whatever was thrown by the owner was a fortune for him.

One day, when he was searching for food, he found a polybag full of eatables near the garbage bin. He didn't understand who had put it there and why, but he was very happy and grateful. After that day, he found polybags of food near the bin regularly. This went on for several years until the owner died. After the owner's death, he stopped finding the bags of food near the garbage bin.

Without that food, it was difficult for him to feed his family on the little salary he earned. So, he went to the owner's wife to ask for a raise. The owner's wife questioned him as to why he hadn't asked for a raise earlier and had been working for such a low salary. He told her about the polybags he used to find every day and how, for that reason, his salary was enough for his family. He further explained that now that he no longer found the bags, he couldn't make ends meet.

The owner's wife had tears in her eyes and said, "My husband used to help everyone he could. Don't worry, you will have the raise."

From the next day, he started to find a polybag with eatables at the same place. This time, he understood that it must be placed by the owner's son. Every day, he would greet the owner's son, but the son never replied to the watchman. One day, fed up with this, the watchman shouted to the owner's son, "Sir, thank you." The owner's son turned around and said, "Sorry, did you say something? I didn't hear you. I have a hearing problem, just like my father did."

Someone may seem arrogant, jealous, or egoistic, but it is always better to first know both sides of every story and then reach any conclusion. You may be right, but you may be wrong as well. We should never be judgemental about a person's character based solely on their behaviour.

Are you sure it is what you think it is?

ACTION TIME

1. How do you feel about the stories?
2. What are your learnings?
3. What things will you do differently from now on and how?

(Please refer to the stories if needed.)

Imagine that you are not yourself but someone else for a day—someone who you know and who knows you. Now, try to write your own story from their perspective or how you would see things as someone else and not yourself.

____

____

____

____

____

____

____

Have you ever been stuck in a traffic jam? Certainly, you have. How do you feel every time you experience it? Now, recollect how you look at a traffic jam/crowded space from the window of your aeroplane seat. Does the view of the bigger picture change how you feel about it?

____

____

____

____

____

HAPPINESS

There is no path to happiness.
Happiness is the path.
Happiness is a choice you need to make every day.
It is crucial not to give others control, and the key to our happiness.

1. Have you ever written down the definition of happiness for yourself—not the one you have believed in all this time because somebody else defined it for you, but your own definition?
2. Have you ever sung a song just for yourself, recorded yourself singing for yourself, danced without anyone watching, gone for a walk/run without caring about the destination, or counted your smiles in a day? Try doing all these things.

53. Are You a '99 Club' Member?

Once upon a time, there lived a king who, despite his luxurious lifestyle, was neither happy nor content. One day, he came upon a servant who was singing happily while he worked. This fascinated the king. He wondered why he, the supreme ruler of the land, was unhappy and gloomy, while a lowly servant was so joyful.

The king asked the servant, "How come you are so happy?"

The man replied, "Your Majesty, I am nothing but a servant. My family and I don't need too much—just a roof over our heads and warm food to fill our tummies."

The king was not satisfied with this reply. Later in the day, he sought the advice of his most trusted advisor. After hearing the king's woes and the servant's story, the advisor said, "Your Majesty, I believe that the servant has not been made part of 'The 99 Club'."

"The 99 Club? What exactly is that?" the king inquired.

The advisor replied, "Your Majesty, to truly know what The 99 Club is, place 99 gold coins in a bag and leave it at this servant's doorstep."

The king did as advised. When the servant saw the bag, he took it into his house. When he opened the bag, he let out a great shout of joy at the sight of so many gold coins. He began to count them. After several counts, he was convinced that there were 99 coins. He wondered, "What could've happened to that last gold coin? Surely, no one would leave 99 coins!"

He looked everywhere but could not find that last coin. Finally, exhausted, he decided that he would work harder than ever to earn that gold coin and complete his collection.

From that day, the servant's life changed. He was overworked, horribly grumpy, and castigated his family for not helping him earn that 100th gold coin. He felt so unhappy all the time that he stopped singing while he worked.

The king was puzzled at this drastic transformation. When he sought his advisor's help, the latter said, "Your Majesty, the servant has now officially joined The 99 Club."

He continued, "The 99 Club is a name given to those people who have enough to be happy but are never content because they're always yearning and striving for that extra 1, telling themselves, "Let me get that one final thing, and then I will be happy for life."

We, too, can be happy with very little in our lives. When we're given something bigger and better, we need to control our monkey minds, which may want even more. We lose our sleep, our happiness, and we hurt the people around us. This is the price we pay for our growing needs and desires.

It is up to us whether we want to join 'The 99 Club' or not.

54. What Made You Happiest in Life?

During a telephonic interview, the radio announcer asked his guest, a millionaire, "What made you happiest in life?"

The millionaire replied, "I have gone through four stages of happiness in life, and finally, I understood the meaning of true happiness. The first stage was of accumulating wealth and means, but I did not get the happiness I wanted. Then came the second stage of collecting valuables and items, but I realized that the satisfaction they provide is also temporary, as the lustre of valuable things does not last long.

"Then came the third stage of acquiring and executing big projects, like buying a football team, a tourist resort, etc. But even here, I did not get the happiness I had imagined.

"Then a friend of mine asked me to buy wheelchairs for some disabled children. At his request, I immediately bought wheelchairs. My friend insisted that I go with him and hand them over to the children. I agreed and gave the wheelchairs to the children with my own hands. I saw the glow of happiness on the faces of these children. I saw them all sitting in wheelchairs, moving around and having fun. It was as if they had arrived at a picnic spot.

"I felt happy and was about to leave when one of the kids grabbed my leg. I gently tried to free myself, but the child held on tightly and stared at my face. I bent down and asked the child, 'Do you need anything else?'

"This child's answer not only made me happy but also changed my life completely. The child said, 'I want to remember your face so that when I meet you in heaven, I will be able to recognize you and thank you once again.'"

Happiness is what we all aim for, but very few of us know what it truly is.

ACTION TIME

1. How do you feel about the stories?
2. What are your learnings?
3. What things will you do differently from now on and how?

(Please refer to the stories if needed.)

Draw a mind map for your happiness. Let each branch represent one thing that makes you happy.

Analyze your mind map, and note how many factors responsible for your happiness are independent of and dependent on external forces. Will you ever be happy if the key lies with something or someone else?

FAITH

Trust the process.
We are all guided by a divine force that seeks nothing but unconditional surrender.
Faith is when you see the invisible,
believe the unbelievable,
and receive the impossible.

1. When a little child is tossed up in the air, he smiles, not cries, because he has faith that his parent will catch him. Isn't this the faith we need to have in the Almighty?
2. When things do not go your way, know that they are going the way the Divine has planned them, and the Divine's plans are always the best! Reflect on how some of the events in your life didn't turn out the way you wanted, and now you are grateful that they didn't.

55. Rain

It was pouring outside, the kind of rain that gushes over the top of rain gutters in such a hurry to hit the earth it has no time to flow down the spout. Several people stood under the shade and just inside the door of the supermarket. They all waited, some patiently, others irritated because nature had disrupted their hurried day.

There was a six-year-old girl among the crowd, a beautiful red-haired, freckle-faced image of innocence.

Her voice was so sweet that it broke the hypnotic trance everyone was caught up in. "Mom, let's run through the rain," she said.

"What?" Mom asked.

"Let's run through the rain," she repeated.

"No, honey. We'll wait until it slows down a bit," Mom replied.

The young child waited about another minute and then repeated, "Mom, let's run through the rain."

"We'll get soaked if we do," Mom said.

"No, we won't, Mom. That's not what you said this morning," the young girl replied as she tugged at her mother's arm.

"This morning? When did I say we could run through the rain and not get wet?"

"Don't you remember? When you were talking to Daddy about his cancer, you said, 'If God can get us through this, he can get us through anything.'"

The entire crowd was silent. Nothing could be heard except the sound of the falling rain.

Mom thought for a moment about what she should say.

Finally, she replied, "Honey, you are absolutely right. Let's run through the rain. If God lets us get wet, maybe we just needed washing."

Then off they ran. Everyone stood watching, smiling, and laughing as they darted past the cars and through the puddles. They held their shopping bags over their heads but got soaked. They were followed by some people who screamed and laughed like children all the way to their cars.

That's what we all need—to live in the moment and to live the moment to the fullest, believing God is watching over us.

God is watching over us.

56. Time to Fly

A man bought two beautiful birds and asked his servant to train them.

After a month, the servant noticed that while one of the birds soared freely into the expanse of the sky, the other remained rooted to a tree branch. The servant tried everything to get the bird to fly. He tried convincing the bird, luring it with food, and even made mock threats, but the bird still hung on firmly to the branch, refusing to budge.

A few days later, the owner arrived to see both birds flying high in the sky. He was puzzled.

"Wasn't that the bird that wouldn't fly? How did you make it fly?" he asked, pointing at the bird.

The servant smiled and replied, "It had no choice. I cut off the branch where the bird was sitting."

We are all made to fly—to realize our incredible potential as human beings. However, instead of doing so, we often sit on our branches, clinging to the things that are familiar to us. Sometimes that's when the Almighty cuts that branch off to push us to take flight.

Let's take a leap of faith; it's time to fly.

57. I Am with You

Every year, a couple took their son to his grandmother's house for the summer break, and they would return home by train after two weeks.

One day, the boy told his parents, "I'm a grown-up now. What if I go to Grandma's house alone this year?"

After a brief discussion, his parents agreed. They went to the railway station to see him off, giving him last-minute instructions through the window. Tired of listening to the instructions, the boy said irritably, "I know, you've already told me so many times!"

The train was about to leave when the father whispered to the boy, "My son, if you suddenly feel bad or scared, this is for you." He slipped a folded piece of paper into his son's pocket.

Now the boy was all alone, sitting in the train, without his parents, for the first time. He looked at the scenic view through the window. Around him, strangers were hustling, making noise, entering and exiting the compartment. Suddenly, the boy noticed a stranger staring at him continuously. The boy felt uncomfortable and also a little scared.

Feeling lonely, he lowered his head and snuggled in a corner of the seat, tears welling up in his eyes. At that moment, he remembered the piece of paper his father had put in his pocket.

With a trembling hand, he took it out and opened it. It read: "Son, don't worry. I am in the next compartment."

The truth is, this is how it is in life. When God sent us into this world, all by ourselves, He also slipped a note in our pocket.

God says: I am travelling with you; I am within your reach. Call on Me!

58. My Father is the Pilot

A priest was on a long flight home after a Church conference. The first warning of approaching problems came when the 'Fasten Your Seat Belts' sign flashed on.

After a while, a calm voice said over the intercom, "We shall not be serving beverages at this time as we are expecting a little turbulence. Please make sure your seat belt is fastened."

The priest looked around the aircraft and saw that many passengers were becoming apprehensive.

Later, the voice over the intercom said, "We are sorry that we are unable to serve meals at this time. The turbulence is still ahead of us."

And then the storm broke.

The ominous cracks of thunder could be heard even above the roar of the engines. Lightning lit up the dark skies, and within moments, the great plane was tossed around like a cork in a celestial ocean. One moment it was lifted on strong currents of air, the next it felt as if about to crash.

As the priest looked around, he could see that all the passengers were alarmed, except one little girl.

She sat calmly, feet tucked under her, looking at pictures in a book, oblivious of the turbulence around her. Sometimes she would close her eyes for a moment and then return to her book.

The storm blew over. When the plane landed and the passengers were disembarking, the priest approached the little girl and asked her why she had not been afraid like the other passengers.

The little girl replied, "Because my Daddy's the pilot, and he's taking me home."

Like the little girl, let us always remember: Our Father is the Pilot.

God is in control. He will take us home. Don't worry!

59. Message from God

A little boy came home from school on a Saturday and told his father, "My teacher has given us homework to smile at 10 people and tell them: 'Be patient, trust life, and I love you.'"

The father said, "Ok, we will go to the mall tomorrow morning and do it."

The child woke up in the morning, got ready, went to his father, and said enthusiastically, "Let's go!"

The father said, "It's raining heavily. I fear nobody might be there."

The child still insisted. So the father drove in the rain to the mall.

They stood in the mall for an hour, and the little boy smiled at nine people. His father then said, "Now let's return. It's raining heavily, and we shouldn't get stuck." Disappointed at not completing his task, the son went along with his father's orders.

As they were driving back home, the child pointed at a random house and said, "Please, Dad, just one person remains. Shall I go to that house and complete my homework?"

The father smiled and pulled the car over.

The child went to the door and began to ring the bell and pound the door with his knuckles. He kept waiting for someone to come.

Finally, the door was opened. A lady came out with a very sad look on her face and gently asked, "What can I do for you, son?"

With radiant eyes and a bright smile, the child said, "Be patient, trust life, and I love you."

He continued, "Ma'am, my teacher has asked me to smile at 10 people and tell them what I just said. I had smiled at 9, and you are the 10th. Thank you!"

The lady embraced him and started crying profusely.

On seeing the lady cry, the boy's father came out of the car. He went to the lady and asked, "Any problem, madam?"

She composed herself, took them inside, served them tea, and then said, "My husband died a while ago, leaving me totally alone in this world. This morning, the loneliness took over me. Since then, I have been thinking that this is the end of the road for me. I took a chair and a rope to my bedroom and decided to end my life. As I was seeing the world for one last time, I begged my Lord for forgiveness and then heard this child's knock.

I thought about ignoring it. But then, nobody comes to visit me. When I opened the door, I couldn't believe my eyes when I saw this little child.

And when he said, 'Be patient, trust life, and I love you', I knew it was a message from God.

Suddenly, I realized I didn't want to die anymore. I have decided to make my life productive."

Be patient. Trust Life. God loves you.

60. Do You Believe in His Existence?

A widow from a poor village in Bengal did not have enough money to pay for her son's bus fare, and so, when the boy started going to school, he would have to walk through the forest alone. To reassure him, she said, "Don't be afraid of the forest, my son. Ask your God, Krishna, to accompany you. He will hear your prayer." The boy followed his mother's suggestion. Krishna duly appeared, and from then on, accompanied him to school every day.

When it was his teacher's birthday, the boy asked his mother for some money to buy him a present. "We haven't any money, son. Ask your brother, Krishna, to get you a present."

The following day, the boy explained his problem to Krishna, who gave him a jug of milk. The boy proudly handed the milk to the teacher, but the other boys' presents were far superior, and the teacher didn't even notice his gift. "Take that jug of milk to the kitchen," said the teacher to an assistant.

The assistant did as he was told. However, when he tried to empty the jug, he found that it immediately filled up again of its own accord. He informed the teacher, who was amazed and asked the boy, "Where did you get that jug, and how does it manage to stay full all the time?"

"Krishna, the god of the forest, gave it to me," replied the boy.

The teacher, the students, and the assistant all burst out laughing. "There are no gods in the forest. That's pure superstition," said the teacher. "If he exists, let's all go and see him."

The whole group set off. The boy started calling for Krishna, but he did not appear. The boy made one last desperate appeal. "Brother Krishna, my teacher wants to see you. Please show yourself!"

At that moment, a voice echoed throughout the forest. "How can he possibly want to see me, my son? He doesn't even believe I exist!"

Faith leads you to miracles.

61. Everything Happens for the Good

There was once a king who had a wise advisor. The advisor followed the king everywhere, and his favourite advice was: "Everything happens for the good."

One day, the king went hunting and had a little accident. He shot an arrow at his own foot and was injured. He asked the advisor what he thought about the accident, to which the advisor replied, "Everything happens for the good."

The king was upset and ordered his advisor to be put in prison. He then asked his advisor, "Now, what do you think?"

The advisor again replied, "Everything happens for the good." So he remained in prison.

The king later went on another hunting trip, this time without the advisor. The king was captured by some cannibals. He was taken to the cannibals' camp, where he was to be their evening meal. Before he was put into the cooking pot, he was thoroughly inspected. The cannibals saw the wound on the king's foot and decided to throw him back into the jungle. According to the cannibals' tradition, they would not eat anything that was imperfect. As a result, the king was spared. He suddenly realized the truth behind his advisor's words. The advisor also escaped death because had he not been in prison, he would have followed the king on the hunting trip and would have ended up in the cooking pot.

Everything happens for a good reason.

ACTION TIME

1. How do you feel about the stories?
2. What are your learnings?
3. What things will you do differently from now on and how?

(Please refer to the stories if needed.)

The future is uncertain. Things may or may not turn out the way you want. Then why stress yourself? Why not just leave it on the Almighty once you have done what you could and let things take their course?

Write down 5 things that concern you the most at present and see if they really are in your control. If not, why not pray to the Almighty to take care of them all?

____

____

____

____

____

GRATITUDE

The ability to breathe is a gift. Wake up grateful each day for that gift.
Gratitude emanates from the realization of the true value of the things, people, and abilities we are blessed with.

1. Being born as a human is, in itself, a Black Swan event! According to Hindu mythology, after 84 lakh *yonis*, one is born as a human. According to science, a human is the most evolved being. Today, we are living the most comfortable lives in the history of humankind.
   Aren't these enough reasons to be grateful every day?
2. There will always be someone prettier, healthier, wealthier, wiser, better…and the fun fact is, this stands true for every single human being on the planet. Each one of us has something missing, and the unfortunate part is that we only focus on that missing piece. What about all that we already have? Shouldn't we be thankful for all that we are blessed with?

62. Magic Box

One pleasant morning, Archie woke up with a startling flash of light, and lo and behold! God was standing before her with two boxes, which He handed to her.

He said, "Put all your sorrows in the black box and all your joys in the gold one."

She heeded His words, and in the two boxes, both her joys and sorrows she stored. However, though the gold one became heavier each day, the black one remained as light as before.

With curiosity, she opened the black one to find out the reason for this, and she saw, at the base of the box, a hole, through which her sorrows had all bid her goodbye. She showed the hole to God, and mused, "I wonder where my sorrows could be!"

He smiled gently and said, "My child, they're all here with me."

She asked God, "Why did you give me the black box with a hole and the gold one without?"

"My child, the gold one is for you to count your blessings, while the black one is not meant to store; it is to let out."

The blessings are what you should count.

63. The Cobbler who also Mends Souls

There was a cobbler who sat across the street in front of Ashna's office building. Every day, she noticed there was a stray dog that came and sat with him as soon as he arrived at the place, and the cobbler fed him biscuits and sometimes milk.

The man would then go on with his work, and the dog would sit there, giving him company. One could feel there was a connection between them, and that, unknown to everyone, they conversed, without a word being spoken.

The cobbler also brought food for birds, which he kept at different places on the street pavement where he sat for his work.

Many people would stop and ask him for directions, and he always showed them the way with a smile, even if he didn't get any business from them.

If he saw a homeless person passing by, he would offer them water and food that he brought for himself and engage in conversations with them. One could see and feel the peace the conversations brought to them.

Ashna felt an inexplicable urge to go and meet him, and she did. He smiled at her and told her his name was Dayaram. He asked her if she would like to have tea.

Pleasantly surprised, she said, "Sure, let's have some tea."

This man, who struggled to make Rs. 100 a day, happily spent around Rs. 25-30 on others. He was rich at heart if not in what he owned, and this abundance that he held in his heart was infectious.

Ashna told him she had been observing him and what he did, and that she was humbled and fascinated by it. She referred to the dog, and he said, "Oh! He's just one of us—God's own creation."

He went on to say that he was not serving anyone; it was the Almighty who was making it happen via him. It would be egoistic to say that he was doing it.

Ashna folded her hands, bowed to him, and requested him to accept some money, saying, "It is not I who is giving you this money; it is the Almighty who is sending it to you via me."

They both laughed, and he accepted the money. As she was about to leave, he said, "Ask from the Almighty, but then don't just accumulate it. Give it away to others with happiness and gratitude, and do so silently."

Ask from the Almighty, but then don't just accumulate it. Give it away to others with happiness and gratitude, and do so silently.

64. Two Makes You Happy, Three Robs You of It

One day, Benjamin Franklin, an American philosopher, called out to his little son and gave him an apple. The boy was very happy to receive the apple, and his eyes sparkled with joy. Benjamin gave him another apple, and the boy took it in his other hand. Now, both his little hands were filled with the juicy, red apples.

Benjamin then gave him a third apple. The child was overwhelmed with joy, but as he tried to hold the third apple, all three apples fell to the ground. The child began to cry.

Despite having everything, man continues to crave more. And it is this craving that is the cause of our unhappiness.

Let's be grateful for what we have and not just focus on what we can or could have.

ACTION TIME

1. How do you feel about the stories?
2. What are your learnings?
3. What things will you do differently from now on and how?

(Please refer to the stories if needed.)

Visit a cancer hospital, an orphanage, or an old-age home. Talk to the kids/people there, hear about their journeys and struggles, and when you return, think about what you are blessed with.

UNCOMPLICATE

Keep it simple, Silly!
Sometimes the simplest things in life are the ones that bring us the most peace.
Life isn't as difficult and complicated as we make it. Our assumptions, biases, presumptions, notions, predictions, and what ifs make it so.

1. Life isn't always supposed to be a trick question. Simplify your vision, and remember that the solution to a problem is born with it. This is nature's law. Think about it.
2. Remember not to confuse simplicity with ease. The answer to your most pressing concern can simply be hard work, but that does not mean this simple solution will be easy to achieve. Ponder this: 'Life is simple but never easy.'

65. How to Excel in the Art of Living

A king once built a very beautiful palace, and at the main entrance, he got his workers to engrave a very difficult mathematical problem. He then announced a 7-day competition, stating that the problem would have to be solved to open the main gate of the palace. Anyone who was successful in opening the gate would be the future heir to the kingdom, as the king did not have any children of his own.

All this was done because he was eager to find a smart and suitable candidate to whom he could pass on the responsibility of running the kingdom well.

After hearing the announcement, all the learned scholars and mathematicians of the kingdom came to the main entrance of the palace and tried to solve the equation, but they had never come across such a difficult problem in their entire lives and returned dejectedly.

Soon, it was the last date of the competition, and three people came to the king, willing to attempt to solve the problem. Two of these were well-known mathematicians from the neighbouring kingdom, and one was a poor farmer belonging to the same kingdom.

The mathematicians applied several formulae to resolve the equation but were unable to find the answer. Finally, the farmer was asked to try his luck. The crowd was restless and not very hopeful about the farmer's chances of opening the gate. "When such learned scholars could not find the answer, what could he do?" they wondered.

The farmer walked towards the main gate to read the mathematical problem but couldn't follow any of it. Finally, he stood by the door and looked at it carefully for a while. A few moments later, he just pushed the door slightly.

To everybody's surprise, the door opened! Everyone was awestruck by his smartness and applauded him for being able to open the gate. The king honoured him and asked him, "What formula did you apply to open the door?"

The farmer humbly replied, "I thought that since the last six days, the most brilliant and learned men tried several formulae to open the gate, but none of them succeeded, so there was something wrong with the problem itself. I also noticed that there was no lock or latch on the gate. So I thought, 'Let's see what the problem is first, and then we can go ahead and solve the question.' The task was to open the door, and so I found the solution."

Several times in life, the 'problem' is not what we think it is, and just the thought of the problem scares us. Our overthinking it further complicates it and makes it tougher to solve. Problems in life are a 'part of living', and facing these challenges with courage and overcoming them is the 'art of living'.

If you open the doors to your mind, all worries will disappear.

66. How Do We Survive?

Once, a very famous author received through the post three litres of a product intended to provide a substitute for milk. A Norwegian company wanted to know if he was interested in investing in the production of this new kind of food because, in the opinion of the expert, 'All cows' milk contains 59 active hormones, a great deal of fat, cholesterol, dioxins, bacteria, and viruses.' Naturally, this new product was plant-based, and milk is condemned on the basis of innumerable studies carried out by various institutes dotted around the world. This got the author pondering where we are headed!

That same afternoon, his wife emailed him an article she had found on the internet, and it is for all of us to read and consider if we are overcomplicating things to set everything right, and our overprotective approach is ultimately doing more harm than good.

The article read: 'People who are now aged between 40 and 60 years old used to drive around in cars with no seat belts, no head support, and no airbags. Children sat in the back, making a tremendous ruckus and having a great time. Baby cribs were painted with brightly coloured paints that contained lead or some other dangerous substance. There was a generation that used to make their own 'go-karts' and race down the hills, using their feet as brakes, falling off, hurting themselves, but very proud of their high-speed adventures. There were no mobile phones, and so our parents had no way of knowing where we were—how was that possible? As children, we were never right. We were occasionally punished, but we never had any psychological problems about feeling rejected or unloved. At school, there were good pupils, and there were bad pupils: the good pupils moved up to the next year, the bad ones flunked. Psychotherapists were not called in to study their case—the bad pupils simply had to repeat the year. And even so, we managed to survive with a few grazed knees and a few traumas. We not only survived, but we look back nostalgically on the days when milk was not a poison, when a child was expected to resolve any problems without outside help, getting into fights if necessary, and spending much of the day without any electronic toys and, instead, inventing games with friends!'

The author thought to himself, "Probably life was more beautiful when it was simpler."

Let's try to simplify, to be closer to what's organic.

67. In the Blue Mountains

Once, a tourist visited a natural park close to Sydney in Australia. There, in the midst of the forest that covered an area known as the Blue Mountains, were three rock formations in the form of obelisks. The tourist, intrigued by the sight, asked his guide what those three rocks were. "They're the Three Sisters," the guide replied and then narrated the age-old legend: "A shaman was out walking with his three sisters when the most famous warrior of the time approached them and said, 'I want to marry one of these lovely girls.' 'If one of them marries, the other two will think they're ugly. I'm looking for a tribe where warriors are allowed to have three wives,' replied the shaman, moving off. For years, the shaman travelled the Australian continent but never found that tribe. 'At least one of us could have been happy,' said one of the sisters, when they were old and tired out from all the walking. 'I was wrong,' said the shaman, 'but now it's too late.' And he transformed the three sisters into blocks of stone, so that anyone who passed by there would understand that the happiness of one does not mean the unhappiness of others.

Remember, to move up in life, it's not necessary to bring someone down.

ACTION TIME

1. How do you feel about the stories?
2. What are your learnings?
3. What things will you do differently from now on and how?

(Please refer to the stories if needed.)

Read this beautiful quote and implement it in life:

Missing somebody? … Call
Wanna meet up? … Invite
Wanna be understood? … Explain
Have questions? … Ask
Don't like something? … Say it
Like something? … State it
Want something? … Ask for it
Love someone? … Tell it
Nobody will know what's going on in your mind.
It's better to express rather than to expect.
You already have the NO,
Take the risk of getting a yes.
We just have one life, keep it simple!

SUCCESS

Success is to each its own!
Yes, it emanates from liking oneself, liking what one does, and liking how one does it...
Success cannot be defined by others for you; it is you who has to define it for yourself.

1. List your parameters of success—your parameters, not those the world tells you.
2. Do you think Mother Teresa was a successful woman? What legacy did she leave behind?

68. Law of Life

When a newspaper reporter interviewed a farmer who won an award for the maize he grew every year and entered in the Agricultural Show, it was revealed that the farmer shared his seed with his neighbours.

Perplexed, the reporter asked, "How can you afford to share your best seed with your neighbours when they are entering their maize in competition with yours each year?"

The farmer smiled and explained, "The wind picks up pollen from the ripening maize and swirls it from field to field. If my neighbours grow inferior maize, cross-pollination will steadily degrade the quality of my maize. If I am to grow good maize, I must help my neighbours grow a good crop."

So is the case with our lives. Those who want to live meaningfully and well must help enrich the lives of others. And those who choose to be happy must help others find happiness.

For, the value of a life is measured by the lives it touches. The welfare of each is bound with the welfare of all.

Call it the power of collectivity, a principle of success, or a law of life.

None of us truly wins until we all win.

69. Navigate Your Future

A young man once went to a fortune teller to enquire about his future. The fortune teller drew two circles, one in white and the other in black. He then put a millipede (an insect) in between the circles, saying, "If the millipede crawls into the white circle, your future will be bright and great, but if it crawls into the black circle, you are finished and doomed! No future at all!"

As soon as the insect was dropped in between the circles, it began crawling towards the white circle. The young man was extremely excited.

But suddenly, as it got to the edge of the circle, the insect turned back and began crawling away from the white circle towards the black one. The man watched as the insect progressively moved farther away from his fortune to his doom. Then, just when the insect got to the edge of the black circle, the man stretched out his hand, picked it up, and quickly but carefully dropped it in the white circle.

The fortune teller was surprised as he had never seen anyone do anything like this. He asked the man why he did so.

The man smiled and replied, "I cannot sit and watch my destiny go down the gloomy doom while I can still do something to change its course. My destiny is in my hands."

It's you who is responsible.

70. Let's Go Fly a Kite

It was a week after the funeral. Sumitra had buried her hardworking accountant husband, who had painstakingly worked from morning till sundown, risen from clerk to bank manager, sent two children to college and made them capable of getting jobs abroad with a coveted income, and given her a comfortable lifestyle.

While organizing her late husband's room, she rummaged in his cupboard, looking for documents and files he had meticulously kept, and it was then that she saw the secret compartment. She did not want to find out any secret about her husband or anything that would tarnish her memories of the solid, dependable, hardworking man he'd been, but she opened the compartment with trembling hands. She felt something light and papery to the touch, then slowly, carefully, pulled out, not one, not two, but a dozen kites. They were crisp as if just bought from the kite shop down the road.

She started weeping when she saw them. "One day," he had told her, "I'll have time to fly kites on the terrace."

"You seem to have flown them before," she had said.

"I loved them when I was little," he had said. "I loved the feel of the kite in the heavens, rising up and reigning like a king!"

"Why don't you do so this Sunday?" she had asked.

"Overtime," he had replied. "But maybe next Sunday or the holiday after that."

She wept as she felt the crisp paper. She wept as the kites spoke a dream of a dead man, who'd wanted the simple pleasure of flying them in the sky.

Her sons came home the next day. They saw the kites affixed to the wall of the sitting room. "Ma," they protested, "this is not the time to celebrate; it is a time of mourning."

"Yes," she said, "I know it is, and that is why I've put them there."

They felt the paper, stared at the lovely designs, and listened to their mother as she told them where she'd found them. They had tears in their eyes as they thought of their father and the kites he'd never flown.

"Ma, I'd like to take one home," said her eldest.

"And I want one for my home, too," said the second.

She gave the kites to them.

They called her the next week. "We're picking you up, Ma. We're going to spend the weekend camping."

"Camping?" she asked. "I've never camped before."

"Nor have we, but that's the kite we want to fly, Ma. Come along!"

She smiled as they drove down the mountain track. She turned to look at her second son's car behind. As she looked out of the window, she felt she could see her husband, laughing as he flew a kite, higher and higher into the wind, reigning like a king. His sad kites in the cupboard had made his sons fly theirs!

Are your kites going to be found in your cupboard, or do they fly in the sky?

Go fly your kite!

71. Have You Made It to the Top?

This is one incident Mohan can never forget. Mohan held a senior consultant position in HR and had just finished his annual reviews. He had the list of employees who were to be given their promotion letters.

All was going well until he called this man to talk to him about a new opportunity. It was a promotion from his current role, and he had the right skills and qualifications. "Sorry, but I'm not interested," he politely said.

Mohan pressed him until the man said something that really confused him. The man said that he had "already made it to the top". Mohan was familiar with his current role and looked at his CV again. He wasn't anywhere near the top. In fact, he wasn't even a Senior Manager yet.

The man explained to Mohan that "making it to the top", for him, meant he loved the work he did each day, he loved his company, he was treated fairly and with respect, he made enough money to be comfortable, he had excellent benefits, he had flexibility, and most importantly to him, he never missed a single football game, school play, parent-teacher conference, anniversary, birthday, or any family event. He knew what taking the next step in his career meant—more time at work, more travel, and sacrifices. "It's not worth it," he said.

Your definition of "making it to the top" doesn't have to be society's or anyone else's definition. We all live with an aspiration to make it to the top. The secret is that it is in your hands to do it. The only thing needed is your vision to define what the "top" is for you.

Life has become a race, and in this, we have forgotten to live life. The sad part is that by the time we want to live, it's too late. We often argue and justify ourselves by saying that we are working hard for the family, to give our kids a good future. But the reality is that if we cannot enjoy time with our loved ones while they are still there, what is the point of it? So here's wishing you the best in life as you make it to the "TOP" in every walk of life.

Your definition of "making it to the top" doesn't have to be society's or anyone else's definition.

ACTION TIME

1. How do you feel about the stories?
2. What are your learnings?
3. What things will you do differently from now on and how?

(Please refer to the stories if needed.)

Define the term 'successful' for yourself, not how the world tells you but how you think success should be defined.

____

____

____

____

____

____

____

____

Write down the steps you will take to achieve your own definition of success.

____

____

____

____

____

____

____

____

____

THE TRUE TREASURE

You have a treasure within you that is infinitely greater than anything the world can offer.
We all decide our treasures based on who we are and what holds the most value for us. Little do we realize that most valuables cannot be bought or traded for money.

1. Alexander the Great won over the world and its riches and yet could not buy himself time or health to meet his beloved one last time. He wanted the world not to repeat his mistake and thus asked his coffin to be made such that his empty hands were visible to the whole world when he departed. Ask yourselves, what will be those 5 things you can take with you at the end of your journey?
2. Remember the Covid times? Be it the first lockdown or the dreaded second wave, there was something that the pandemic taught us all. Locked inside our houses, surrounded by our loved ones, with the basic availability of food, shelter, and clothing, we all felt secure and happy. It wasn't the fear of losing money but our loved ones, our precious lives, that concerned us the most. There were people ready to give away all their wealth and property to just find one bed in the hospital or be able to see their loved ones for one last time, but to no avail. What has been your biggest lesson?

72. Are You Pouring Milk or Water?

Once, a Gram Panchayat asked some workers to dig a pond and made a public announcement that they wanted to create a pool filled with milk. They asked one person from each household to bring a glass of milk at night and pour it into the pond so that it would be filled with milk by the morning.

As one man was preparing to go to the pond, he decided to instead take just a glass of water and pour it into the pond. He thought that since everybody else would bring milk, his act would go unnoticed due to the dark of the night.

So he quickly went to the pond, poured water into it, and returned home quietly. When the Gram Panchayat visited the pond the next morning, they were surprised to see nothing but water in it. Everyone in the village had thought like the man: "I don't have to put in milk. Someone else will do it."

Don't we also often behave like the people in this village? We tend to believe that someone else will do the job, and we need to only support it without actually doing anything.

Let's take personal responsibility for the tasks assigned to us and not completely depend on others. Integrity is the most precious possession.

73. Can You Sleep When the Wind Blows?

Years ago, a farmer owned land along the Atlantic coast. He constantly advertised for hired hands. Most people were reluctant to work on farms along the Atlantic. They dreaded the awful storms that raged across the Atlantic, wreaking havoc on the buildings and crops. As the farmer interviewed applicants for the job, he received a steady stream of refusals.

Finally, a short, thin man, well past middle age, approached the farmer. "Are you a good farm hand?" the farmer asked him.

"Well, I can sleep when the wind blows," answered the short man.

Although puzzled by this answer, the farmer, desperate for help, hired him. The man worked well around the farm, busy from dawn to dusk, and the farmer felt satisfied with his work.

Then one night, the wind howled loudly from offshore.

Jumping out of bed, the farmer grabbed a lantern and rushed next door to the hired hand's sleeping quarters. He shook the man and yelled, "Wake up! A storm is coming! Tie things down before they blow away!"

The man rolled over in bed and said firmly, "No, sir. I told you, I can sleep when the wind blows."

Enraged by the response, the farmer was tempted to fire him on the spot. Instead, he hurried outside to prepare for the storm.

To his amazement, he discovered that all of the haystacks had been covered with tarpaulins. The cows were in the barn, the chickens were in the coops, and the doors were barred. The shutters were tightly secured. Everything was tied down. Nothing could blow away.

The farmer then understood what his hired hand meant, so he returned to his bed to sleep as well while the wind blew.

When we are prepared, spiritually, mentally, and physically, we have nothing to fear.

Can you sleep when the wind blows through your life?

The above story talks about trials and tribulations in life, and if we do our best to understand, accept, and implement the principles learned by us, we will experience a deep sense of security, peace, and joy from within. We will then be able to sleep when the wind blows.

Can you sleep when the wind blows through your life?

74. State of Mind

Murugan, the proprietor of a coffee shop, had been busy all day. Being Saturday, his shop was very crowded, and the customers seemed endless. He had been on his feet since morning. Towards the evening, he felt the beginning of a splitting headache.

As the clock ticked away the hours, his headache worsened. Unable to bear it, he stepped out of the shop, leaving his staff to look after the sales. He walked across the street to the pharmacy to buy himself a painkiller to relieve his headache. He swallowed the pill and felt relieved. He knew that, in a few minutes, he would feel better.

As he strolled out of the shop, he casually asked the salesgirl, "Where is Mr Gopalan, the chemist? He's not at the cash counter today."

The girl replied, "Sir, Mr Gopalan had a splitting headache and said he was going across to your coffee shop. He said a cup of hot coffee would relieve him of his headache."

The man's mouth went dry, and he mumbled, "Oh, I see!"

How strange, but true! The chemist relieves his headache by drinking coffee, and the coffee shop owner finds relief in a pain-relieving pill!

This is a typical case of looking outside ourselves for something we have within us. Similarly, many of us travel across the length and breadth of the universe and also visit several shrines and ashrams to find peace.

Eventually, we come to realize that real peace lies within our own hearts.

It all lies within.

75. Nothing More than a Burden

One morning, Ravi wasted nearly an hour watching a tiny ant carry a huge feather across its back on the terrace. Several times, it was confronted with obstacles in its path, and after a momentary pause, it would make the necessary detour.

At one point, the ant had to negotiate a crack in the concrete about 10mm wide. After brief contemplation, the ant laid the feather over the crack, walked across it, picked up the feather on the other side, and then continued on its way.

Ravi was fascinated by the ingenuity of this ant, one of God's smallest creatures. It served to reinforce the miracle of creation. Here was a minute insect, lacking in size yet equipped with a brain to reason, explore, discover, and overcome. But this ant, like its two-legged co-residents of this planet, also has human failings.

After some time, the ant finally reached its destination—a flower bed at the end of the terrace and a small hole that was the entrance to its underground home. And it was here that the ant finally met its match.

How could that large feather possibly fit down that small hole? Of course, it couldn't. So the ant, after going through all this trouble, exercising great ingenuity, and overcoming problems along the way, just abandoned the feather and went home.

The ant had not thought the problem through before it began its epic journey, and in the end, the feather was nothing more than a burden.

Isn't life like that? We worry about money or the lack of it, work, where we live, name, fame, and all sorts of things.

These are all burdens, things we pick up along life's path and lug around the obstacles and over the crevasses that life will bring, only to find that at the destination, they are useless, and we can't take them with us.

Check if what you are chasing is nothing more than a burden.

76. The Diamond

A *sanyasi* had reached the outskirts of a village and settled down under a tree for the night when a villager came running to him and said, "The stone! The stone! Give me the precious stone!"

"What stone?" asked the *sanyasi*.

"Last night, Lord Shiva appeared to me in a dream," said the villager. "He told me that if I went to the outskirts of the village at dusk, I would find a *sanyasi* who would give me a precious stone that would make me rich forever."

The *sanyasi* rummaged in his bag and pulled out a stone. "He probably meant this one," he said as he handed the stone over to the villager. "I found it on a forest path some days ago. You can certainly have it."

The man gazed at the stone in wonder. It was a diamond, probably the largest diamond in the whole world.

He took the diamond and walked away. All night, he tossed about in bed, unable to sleep. The next day, at the crack of dawn, he woke the *sanyasi* up and said, "Give me the wealth that makes it possible for you to give this diamond away so easily."

Have we ever thought about it? What is the one thing that belongs only to us and can never be stolen, the one thing that makes us realize our real worth against that of all material things?

Discover for yourself that which you would not trade for anything.

77. Beauty vs Behaviour

A Zen master, while giving a discourse, asked a 35-year-old married man to stand up and said to him, "You are walking on a beach, and a young, beautiful girl is coming towards you. What will you do?"

The man replied, "I will look at her and admire her personality."

The master asked, "After that girl has moved forward, will you look back, too?"

The man answered, "Yes, if my wife is not with me."

Everyone laughed.

The master again asked, "Tell me, how long will you remember that beautiful face?"

The man replied, "Maybe for 5-10 minutes, until another beautiful face appears," and smiled.

The master then said to him, "Now just imagine: When you are going from here, I will give you a packet of books and say that the packet should be delivered to a great, rich person around 75 kilometres away from your home. You go to his house to deliver the books. When you see his house, you realize he is a billionaire. There are 10 vehicles parked in the porch of his bungalow and five watchmen standing outside the house. You send the information of your arrival with the books inside, and then that gentleman himself comes out and greets and welcomes you. He takes the books from you. Then, when you start to leave the place, you are requested very humbly by him to come inside his home. He sits beside you and serves you hot tea and food. He takes very good care of you and thanks you for having delivered the books to him so soon.

"While you are leaving, he asks you, 'How did you come to my house?' You say, 'By the local train.' Immediately, he asks his driver to take you to your destination in one of his luxurious cars, and as soon as you are about to reach your place, that billionaire gentleman makes a call to you and asks, 'Brother, have you reached comfortably?'"

The master asked the man again, "Now tell me, how long will you remember this gentleman?"

The man replied, "Sir, I will never forget that person in my life for his humble and warm behaviour despite him being a billionaire."

Addressing the gathering, the master said, "This is the reality of life. A beautiful face is remembered for a short time, but beautiful behaviour is remembered a lifetime."

Concentrate on the beauty of your behaviour more than that of your face and body. Life will become enjoyable for you and unforgettably beautiful and inspirational for others.

It's not in the face but in the heart.

78. Eating the Cookie

A successful businessman once shared that before he was diagnosed with cancer, he would become depressed if things did not go a certain way. Happiness was 'having the cookie'. If you had the cookie, things were good. If you didn't have the cookie, life wasn't worth anything. Unfortunately, the cookie kept changing. Sometimes it was money, sometimes power. At other times, it was a new car, the biggest contract, the most prestigious address, etc.

A year and a half after his diagnosis of prostate cancer, he sat shaking his head ruefully. He said, "It was like I had stopped learning how to live after I was a kid. When I give my son a cookie, he is happy. If I take the cookie away or it breaks, he is unhappy. But he is two and a half years old, and I am 43. It's taken me this long to understand that the cookie will never make me happy for long. The minute you have the cookie, it starts to crumble, or you start to worry about it crumbling or about someone trying to take it away from you. You have to give up a lot of things to take care of the cookie, to keep it from crumbling and make sure that no one takes it away from you. You may not even get a chance to eat it because you are so busy just trying not to lose it. Having the cookie is not what life is about."

He then laughed and said that cancer changed him. For the first time, he was happy, regardless of whether or not his business was doing well or he won or lost at golf.

He said, "Two years ago, cancer asked me, 'Okay, what's important? What is truly important?' Well, life is important, anyway you can have it. Life with the cookie. Life without the cookie. Happiness does not have anything to do with the cookie; it has to do with being alive." He paused and added thoughtfully, "I guess life is the cookie."

Enjoy this cookie of life before it's too late.

ACTION TIME

1. How do you feel about the stories?
2. What are your learnings?
3. What things will you do differently from now on and how?

(Please refer to the stories if needed.)

What is valuable? Here is a list for you to analyze, if the following can be counted as treasures:

- Your ability to read and understand this book
- The innocent smile of all the young ones in your family
- The blessings and care of elders you receive in numerous forms, even when they are scolding you
- The ability to feel happiness, sorrow, and all other emotions that make you human
- The faith and hope with which you sleep every night that you will witness the new day tomorrow
- Your perseverance and strength that has always kept you going in all difficult situations
- Having someone who loves you deeply
- Your body that is running smoothly and supporting you in all your endeavours
- Your sight that lets you embrace the beauty of this world

The list above might have seemed a little strange in the beginning, but if you have thought deeply enough, you will realize that these are indeed treasures we often take for granted. List some more such treasures that you can think of in the space below:

FAMILY

Humans are social animals and thus cannot survive alone. We need our families (biological or chosen) to sail through life. Other things may change, but we start and end with our families.
During both the best and the worst of our days, all we yearn for is our families.

1. Recollect one of the fondest memories of your life so far, and check who you were around or with. Why is it your fondest memory?
2. Like any other family, you, too, must have had moments of disagreement, contention, or disappointment with your loved ones, but if you dig deep, you will realize they always stem from love, concern, or care. Do that for yourself.

79. Be the Bee

One day, Andrew visited his father, who lived in the countryside. His father kept bees, and he showed Andrew the honey he had collected from the hives.

He took the lid off a five-gallon bucket full of honey, and on top of the honey, there were three little bees, struggling. They were covered in sticky honey and drowning. Andrew asked his father if they could help them, and he replied that they wouldn't survive. In his opinion, they were casualties of honey collection.

Having learnt from his father to put a suffering animal (or bug) out of its misery, Andrew asked him again if they could at least get them out and kill them quickly. His father finally agreed and scooped the bees out of the bucket. He put them in an empty yoghurt container and placed it outside on a bench.

As Andrew's father had disrupted the hive with the earlier honey collection, there were bees flying all around outside. He called Andrew out a little while later to show him what was happening. These three little bees were surrounded by their sisters (all the bees are females), who were cleaning the sticky, nearly dead bees, helping them get the honey off their bodies.

Andrew and his father came back a short time later to find that there was only one little bee left in the container. She was still being tended to by her sisters.

When it was time for Andrew to leave, they checked one last time. All three bees had been cleaned off enough to fly away, and the container was empty.

Those three little bees survived because they were surrounded by family and friends who would not give up on them, who refused to let them drown in their own stickiness, and who resolved to help until the last one could be set free.

We could all learn a thing or two from these bees.

Bee sisters. Bee peers. Bee teammates.

Be someone's Bee, or be kind enough so that someone bees around you.

80. Sweet Dreams

A young boy and girl were enjoying a pleasant afternoon playing outside in their neighbourhood together. The boy showed the girl his collection of beautiful, unique marbles. In turn, the girl showed the boy the handful of candy she had just got for her birthday. The boy proposed that the two of them exchange their treasures—he would give her all his marbles if she handed over all her candy.

The girl agreed, as she liked the beautiful marbles. The boy handed over his marbles but kept one, the most exquisite of them all, in his pocket. The girl kept her promise and gave the boy all her candy. That night, the girl was happy with the exchange and peacefully went to sleep.

The boy, however, couldn't sleep, as he wondered if the girl had secretly kept some of her candy, just like he had with the marbles.

If you don't give 100 per cent in your relationships, you will always assume your partner isn't giving 100 per cent either. If you want your relationships to be built on trust, you have to be a participating factor in that. The one who is honest will sleep peacefully at night.

What you give is what you get.

81. A Brother Like That

A young man received a trendy car as a Christmas gift from his brother. On Christmas Eve, this young man went for a drive in his new car. After a while, he stopped near a park.

"Is this your car, Mister?" asked a young boy.

The young man nodded with pride. "My brother got me this amazing car for Christmas," he said.

The boy's eyes grew wide in astonishment. "Do you mean your brother got this fantastic car for you, and it didn't cost you anything? How I wish..." the boy hesitated.

The man knew what the little boy wished for. Of course, he would want a brother who gave him such a beautiful car like that. But the boy's words stunned the young man.

"One day, I wish," the boy continued, "I could be a brother just like your brother."

The young man was astounded and impulsively asked, "Would you like to take a ride in my new car?"

"Yes! Yes! I'd love to!" the kid enthusiastically responded. With glowing eyes and a wide smile, he said, "Mister! Would you mind driving to my home?"

The man smiled and agreed. They set off together. The man thought he knew what the young boy wanted—to show kids in the neighbourhood that he could ride home in a fancy car. However, the man was wrong again. On reaching home, the boy ran up the steps. After a while, he returned, carrying his disabled little brother. The young boy pointed at the man's fancy car and said to his brother, "There it is, just like I told you. His brother presented it to him for Christmas, and it didn't cost him a cent. One day, I'm going to give you something like this. Then you will be able to see for yourself all the beautiful Christmas decorations in the windows I've been trying to tell you about."

The young man helped the little brother climb into the car's front seat, and the three of them had a memorable holiday ride.

That day, the man understood the real meaning of the saying: "It is more blessed to give than receive."

It is more blessed to give than receive.

82. The Thread of a Relationship

After the death of a jeweller, his family was in grave trouble. They did not have enough money even for food. One day, his wife gave her son a sapphire necklace and said, "Son, take this to your uncle's shop. Ask him to sell it and give us some money."

The son took the necklace and reached his uncle's shop. His uncle inspected the necklace thoroughly and said, "Son, tell your mother that the market is very low right now. If she sells it after some time, she will get a good price." He gave him some money and further said, "Come and sit with me at the shop from tomorrow."

So, the next day onwards, the boy began going to the shop every day. He started learning how to test diamonds and gems. Soon, he became a well-known connoisseur of diamonds. People would come from far and wide to get their diamonds tested by him.

One day, his uncle said, "Son, bring that necklace from your mother. Tell her that the market is good now, and she will get a handsome price for it."

After taking the necklace from his mother, the young man tested it and found it to be fake. He began to wonder why his uncle, who was such a great connoisseur, hadn't informed them of it. Leaving the necklace at home, he returned to the shop.

His uncle asked, "Didn't you bring the necklace?"

He said, "Uncle, it's not real. But why did you hide this from me?"

His uncle replied, "If I had told you it was fake when you had first brought it to me, you would have thought that I was saying so only because you were in a difficult situation. Today, when you yourself have the knowledge, you know for certain that the necklace is fake. At that time, it was more important for me to take care of our relationship than to speak the truth."

The truth is that, without knowledge, everything we think, see, and know in this world is wrong. And because of this, our relationships become victims of misunderstandings, which then lead to rifts, and our lives start falling apart. The invisible thread by which relationships are tied is strengthened by love and trust.

Don't leave someone's side at the slightest strain in relations. It takes a lifetime to make people your own.

The thread of a relationship is too delicate to be handled without utmost care.

83. A Lesson Well Learnt

A 35-year-old man was getting ready for a Sunday outing with his family. He informed his aged mother, "Amma, I am going to the mall with Usha and Prerna."

"OK, son. My legs are aching. I am not interested in going to the mall. You go ahead," said his mother.

"Grandma, you should also come with us," insisted the granddaughter.

"Prerna, Grandma cannot climb all those steps in the mall. She does not know how to use the escalator. As there are no temples there, Grandma would be bored. She is interested only in going to temples," said Usha.

Though Grandma agreed with this statement, Prerna was adamant. She refused to go to the mall if Grandma did not accompany them. Though Grandma repeated she was not interested, she finally had to comply with her dear ten-year-old granddaughter's will.

Prerna was very happy. The oldest and the youngest of the family were the first ones to get ready. The young child took her grandmother to the front room. She drew two parallel lines, a foot apart, on the floor. She told her grandmother that it was a game, and the old lady had to pretend that she was a crane (the bird). She had to keep one leg within the lines and raise the other leg by three inches.

"What is this, my dear?" asked Grandma.

"This is the crane game, Grandma. I will show you how to play it." Both of them played for a while, and by the time Prerna's father brought the car around, Grandma had become adept at the game.

They reached the mall. At the escalator, the couple wondered how the elderly lady would manage stepping on it. The child took her grandmother near the escalator and asked her to play the crane game. Grandma raised her right foot and placed it on one of the moving steps. Then she raised her left leg by three inches and could easily reach the next moving step. This way, she used the escalator easily to reach the higher level, much to the amazement of her son and daughter-in-law. Then Grandma and her granddaughter moved up and down several times on the escalator and had fun.

They then went to the theatre to watch a movie. It was cold inside. Prema had come prepared for this. She took out a shawl from her bag and covered the old lady. After the movie, they went to a restaurant. When the son asked his mother about the dishes to be ordered, his daughter took the menu from him and thrust it into Grandma's hands. "You know how to read. Go through the menu and order whatever you want." Grandma decided on the dishes to be eaten. After the meal, Grandma and the granddaughter played some video games. Before leaving for home, Grandma went to the washroom.

Taking advantage of her absence, the father asked his daughter how she knew so much about his mother, of which he, as her son, was not aware. "Dad," replied Prerna, "when I was a young child and had to be taken out of the home, you and Mom must have made many preparations—milk bottles, diapers, wipes, etc.. Your mother must have also done the same for you. Why not show the same consideration for your mother? Why did you presume that she would be interested only in temples? The elderly also have normal desires, like spending time with family, going out, and having fun. Since they may not openly express it, we have to compel them to enjoy these things."

The father was speechless. However, he was happy that he had learnt a lesson from his ten-year-old daughter.

A lot goes into making you who you are. We assume many things about elderly parents that are not true. It is called 'generation gap', but it is actually just a matter of perspective and empathy.

Life is about giving back. Do it graciously.

84. Give and Take

Veena was surprised when she heard her father asking their 91-year-old neighbour for some sugar.

She asked her father, "We have sugar at home. Why did you ask our neighbour for it?"

He replied, "It's because he always asks us for stuff; it's hard for him to get things. I ask him for something small so it doesn't burden him, and at the same time, it makes him feel like we need him, too."

He went on, "That way, it'll be much easier for him to ask for anything he needs from us."

This got her thinking and should get us thinking, too. It's not just giving that makes us rich; the act of taking also sometimes needs us to have a big heart.

It's not just giving that makes us rich; the act of taking also sometimes needs us to have a big heart.

85. You Are with Me

It was bedtime, and Rakesh and his wife turned off the lights in the house to help their three-year-old son prepare for bed.

The only light left on was in the room where the three of them were sitting. In a not-yet-tired voice, the son said, "Daddy, I need to go to the washroom." Thankfully, he was finally learning to use the bathroom on his own.

Rakesh said, "OK, you know where the bathroom is." He watched as the little boy skipped to the short hallway leading to the bathroom, only to see him turn and run back to him.

"Daddy, I can't go there. It's dark."

"Then turn the light on," Rakesh said.

"Daddy, it's scary. I want you to come with me," the little boy begged.

With a sigh, Rakesh got up and followed his son as he trotted toward the bathroom.

When they reached the dark hallway, the boy turned to his father and said, "Daddy, put your hands on my shoulders."

Rakesh did as told and followed the boy as he confidently walked on into the darkness. "Why don't you turn the light on?" Rakesh asked.

"It's OK, Daddy," he said. "I don't need to because you're with me."

This made Rakesh think: "To how many people have I given this confidence of being there for them, not merely through my words but even the smallest of gestures? And how many people do I believe are still with me today, even though their past actions have shown me they are always there?"

Let's be there for each other.

86. A Lesson from a Stranger

One night, Sue quarrelled with her mother and then stormed out of the house. En route, she remembered she did not have any money in her pocket, not even enough coins to make a phone call home.

She passed a noodle shop. The aroma wafting from it made her feel very hungry. She wished for a bowl of noodles, but she had no money!

The seller saw her hesitating before the counter and asked, "Hey, little girl, do you want to eat a bowl of noodles?"

"I don't have any money," she shyly replied.

"That's okay, I'll treat you," the seller said. "Come in. I will cook you a bowl of noodles." A few minutes later, the owner brought her a steaming bowl of noodles. While eating, Sue began to cry. "What's wrong?" he asked.

"Nothing. I am just touched by your kindness," Sue said as she wiped her tears. "Even a stranger on the street gives me a bowl of noodles, but my mother, after a quarrel, chased me out of the house. She is cruel!"

The seller sighed, "Girl, why do you think so? I only gave you a bowl of noodles, and you feel indebted. Your mother has raised you since you were little. Why were you not grateful and were disobedient to her?"

Sue realized the truth behind his words. She decided to return home and ask her mother for forgiveness. "On the way back, Sue thought about what she would say to her mother when she reached home: "Mom, I'm sorry. I know it is my fault. Please forgive me."

Once home, Sue found her mother worried and tired from looking for her everywhere. Upon seeing Sue, her mother gently said, "Sue, come inside, honey. You are probably very hungry. I have prepared dinner. Come and eat while it is still hot."

Unable to control her tears any longer, Sue cried in her mother's arms.

Often in life, we find it easy to appreciate the small actions of those around us, but we fail to see the sacrifices of our closest relatives and loved ones, treating their love as a duty or taking it for granted.

Love and concern from our near and dear ones are the most precious gifts, yet we also need to learn to appreciate and cherish the unconditional sacrifices of our loved ones.

If you have a family to call your own, know
that you are blessed. Be grateful.

ACTION TIME

1. How do you feel about the stories?
2. What are your learnings?
3. What things will you do differently from now on and how?

(Please refer to the stories if needed.)

Write a letter of gratitude to your parents or any other family member, stating all that you think you could never thank them enough for. Additionally, mention the moments you wish to apologize for. Tell them how much you love, cherish, and treasure them, even if you fail to express it often.

PARENTING

None has been a perfect parent, nor is, nor will be. Every generation has not only learnt some DON'Ts from the previous one but also picked up some wrong Dos. Each one is a work in progress, learning and unlearning every day.

Parenting isn't about taking the onus of setting everything right for our children, living our dreams through them, or being their biggest critic and harshest ringmaster so that no one else can raise a finger at them.

It is about being the right guide or role model they wish to emulate every day. It is about giving unconditional love and support, while also being courageous enough to present the reality check they need.

1. As parents, we must remember that the hardships of our journey have moulded us into who we are. We must ask ourselves if our endeavour to provide our children the most comfortable lives and fulfil their every need, even before they realize it, is helping them or making their lives ahead more difficult.
2. Are our children and their achievements a matter of competition? Are unrealistic expectations and bizarre comparisons justified as a price for the comfortable lives we bestow on them?

87. From Exclusion to Inclusion

Aryaa had just returned from her trip to Japan, and she couldn't stop praising the country. As a mother of two, she felt as though the 7-day trip to Japan was a crash course on parenting. She had her friend, Ramya, over and was narrating anecdotes about her vacation when Ramya asked her to share one key takeaway from her experience.

Aryaa recounted: Remember the game 'Musical Chairs'? They bring nine chairs for ten children and tell the kids that whoever remains without a chair is out of the game, and the one who gets the last chair is the winner.

Then they reduce the number of chairs each time, and a child comes out of the game every time, until one child remains, and he is declared the winner.

The child learns the culture: 'Myself, myself, and in order to succeed, I must remove others.'

In Japanese kindergartens, they play the game, too. They also bring nine chairs for ten kids. However, there's a difference. They tell the children that if one of them remains without a chair, everyone loses. All the children try to hug each other, so that ten children can sit on nine chairs.

Then they reduce the number of chairs successively, with the rule that they must make sure no one remains without a chair, or else they will all lose.

The child learns the culture: 'I cannot succeed without the help of others.'

We, indeed, cannot succeed without the help of others.

88. Cows Don't Give Milk

A milkman who owned a few cows would say to his young children, "When you all reach the age of 12, I will tell you the secret of life."

One day, when the oldest turned 12, he curiously asked his father about the secret of life.

The father replied, "I will tell you, but don't reveal it to your brothers. The secret of life is: The cow does not give milk."

"What are you saying?" asked the boy incredulously.

"As you hear it, son. The cow does not give milk; you have to milk it. You have to get up at four in the morning, go to the field, walk through the corral full of manure, tie the tail, hobble the legs of the cow, sit on the stool, place the bucket, and do the work yourself."

This is the secret of life. The cow does not give milk. You milk her, or you don't get milk. The younger generation thinks that cows give milk and that things are automatic and free. Their mentality is: "If I wish, I ask, I obtain." They are accustomed to getting whatever they want the easy way. But life is not a matter of wishing, asking, and obtaining.

The things that one receives are the result of the efforts put in. Happiness is the result of effort. Lack of effort creates frustration.

Cows don't give milk. You have to milk the cow for it.

89. I Do Not Help My Wife

On a beautiful Saturday evening, a friend came to Mahesh's house for coffee. They sat and talked about life. At some point during the conversation, Mahesh said, "I'm going to wash the dishes. I'll be right back."

His friend looked at Mahesh as if he had said he was going to build a space rocket.

Then he said, "I'm glad you help your wife. I do not help mine because when I do, she never appreciates me. Last week, I cleaned the floor, but she didn't even thank me."

Mahesh went back to sit with him and explained that he did not 'help' his wife. His wife did not need help; she needed a partner. He said, "I am a partner at home. Society has divided functions, but it is not 'help', as they put it."

"I do not help my wife clean the house because I live here, too, and I need to clean it, too. I do not help my wife to cook because I also want to eat, and I need to cook, too. It is the same with washing dishes, taking care of the children's needs and studies, or washing, hanging, or folding the clothes. I am not a 'help' at home; I am part of this home."

He further asked his friend when was the last time he had praised his wife after she finished cleaning the house, washing clothes, changing bedsheets, bathing the children, cooking, and organising, or when he even just said thank you of the type: 'Wow, sweetheart! You are fantastic!'

He added, "Why not praise her as you wanted to be praised, in the same way, with the same intensity? Give her a hand, and behave like a true companion, not as a guest who only comes home to eat, sleep, bathe, and satisfy needs. Feel at home. That's your home, too."

These thoughts should extend beyond just the spouse or wife. We co-exist everywhere—at home, workplace, neighbourhood, city, and country. True societal change must begin within our homes. Let us not have to teach our sons and daughters the true meaning of responsibility. Instead, let them learn it through our behaviour.

Are you sharing responsibility or doing a favour?

90. What's Your Worth?

Some years ago, three brothers left their farm to work in the city. They were all hired by the same company at the same pay. Three years later, Jim was being paid $500 a month, Frank was receiving $1,000, but George was now making $1,500. Their father decided to visit the employer. He could not understand why the three brothers had different salaries. They were all the same to him. The employer listened to the confused father and said, "I will let the boys explain for themselves."

Jim was summoned to the supervisor's office and was told, "Jim, I understand Far East Importers have just brought in a large transport plane loaded with Japanese goods. Will you please go over to the airport and get a cargo inventory?"

Three minutes later, Jim returned to the office. "The cargo was 1,000 bolts of Japanese silk," he reported. "I got the information over the telephone from a member of the crew."

When Jim left, Frank, the $1,000-a-month brother, was called. "Frank," said the supervisor, "I want you to go to the airport and get an inventory of the cargo plane which was just brought in by Far East Importers."

An hour later, Frank was back in the office with a list showing that the plane carried 1,000 bolts of Japanese silk, 500 transistor radios, and 1,000 hand-painted bamboo trays.

George, the $1,500-a-month brother, was given identical instructions. Working hours were over when he finally returned. "The transport plane carried 1,000 bolts of Japanese silk," he began. "It was on sale at $60 a bolt, so I took a two-day option on the whole lot. I have wired a designer in New York, offering the silk at $75 a bolt. I expect to have the order tomorrow. I also found 500 transistor radios, which I sold over the telephone at a profit of $2.30 each. There were 1000 bamboo trays, but they were of poor quality, so I didn't try to do anything with them."

When George left the office, the employer smiled. "You probably noticed," he said, "that Jim doesn't do what he's told, Frank does only what he's told, but George does without being told."

All children are the same to their parents, but that does not mean they have the same capabilities. Let each blossom into who they are.

91. The Plant that Survived

Once upon a time, there were two neighbours. One of them was a retired teacher, and the other was an insurance agent who was very interested in technology. Both of them had planted different plants in their garden. The retired teacher gave a small amount of water to his plants and didn't always give his full attention to them, while the other neighbour watered his plants too much and looked after them too well.

The retired teacher's plants were simple but looked good. The insurance agent's plants were much fuller and greener. One night, there was a minor storm with heavy rain. The next morning, both neighbours came out to inspect the damage to their garden. The insurance agent saw that his plants had been uprooted and were completely destroyed. However, the retired teacher's plants were not damaged at all and were standing firm.

The insurance agent was surprised to see this, so he went to the retired teacher and asked, "We both grew plants together. I looked after my plants better than you did yours and even gave them more water. Still, my plants were uprooted, while yours were not. How is that possible?"

The retired teacher smiled and replied, "You gave your plants more attention and water, but because of that, they didn't need to work for water themselves. You made it easy for them. I gave them just an adequate amount of water and let their roots search for more. And, because of that, their roots went deeper, which made them stronger. That is why my plants survived."

Are you making your children's roots stronger?

ACTION TIME

1. How do you feel about the stories?
2. What are your learnings?
3. What things will you do differently from now on and how?

(Please refer to the stories if needed.)

Write down all the practices that you tell your children to stay away from and yet, often or seldom, do yourself.

____

____

____

____

____

____

____

____

____

List your 5 most significant duties as a parent. Once you are done, verify the same with your kids and check if you are on the same page (make sure the child knows that fulfilling material wishes does not count).

____

____

____

____

____

____

____

____

PATCHWORK OF WISDOM

Not every life lesson can be tied to a theme, not every experience can be put in a box.
Some tales are precious because of their wisdom. To each, its own.
The stories you read here contain valuable lessons to learn, but it is your choice to determine which one it will be.

92. Seeds of Truth

Long ago, the kingdom of Mewar was ruled by a just and generous emperor. All the people in the kingdom were happy and satisfied with their king, but he was growing old, and his subjects were worried about who would be his heir.

The king knew it was time to choose his successor. He called all the young people in the kingdom together and said, "The time has come for me to step down. I have decided to choose the next emperor from among you. I will give each of you a seed. It is a very special seed. I want you to go home, plant the seed, water it, and come back here one year from today with the plant you have grown from this one seed. I will then judge the plants that you bring to me, and the one I choose will be the next emperor of the kingdom."

Among the group was a boy named Shambhu. He, too, received a seed. He went home, planted the seed, and watered it carefully. Every day, he would check if it had grown. After about three weeks, the others in the group began talking about their seeds and the plants that were beginning to grow. Shambhu kept checking his pot, but nothing ever grew.

Six months went by, but still nothing grew in Shambhu's pot.

After a year, the young people brought their plants to the emperor for inspection. "My goodness! What great plants, trees, and flowers you have grown," said the emperor. "Today, one of you will be appointed the next emperor!"

All of a sudden, he spotted Shambhu at the back of the room, carrying his empty pot. He ordered his guards to bring Shambhu to the front. The boy was terrified.

Just when Shambhu thought he was in trouble, the emperor announced to the crowd, "Behold your new emperor!"

Shambhu couldn't believe it. He hadn't grown anything.

How could he be the new emperor?

Then the emperor said, "One year ago today, I gave everyone here a seed. All of you, except Shambhu, have brought me trees, plants, and flowers. The truth is, I gave you all boiled seeds which would not grow. When you found that the seed would not grow, you substituted it. Shambhu was the only one with the courage and honesty to bring me a pot with my seed in it. Therefore, he is the one who will be the new emperor."

Taking unfair shortcuts may give us short-term results, but in the long run, we may end up losing more than we gain.

Integrity comes with its own rewards. Let's try to stick to our principles and work with integrity.

93. Why do we SHOUT in ANGER?

A saint asked his disciples, "Why do we shout in anger? Why do people shout at each other when they are upset?"

The disciples thought for a while, then one of them said, "We shout for the calm we lose."

"But why shout when the other person is just next to you?" asked the saint. "Isn't it possible to speak to them in a soft voice?"

The disciples gave different answers, but none satisfied the saint.

He then explained, "When two people are angry at each other, their hearts become distant. To cover that distance, they must shout to be able to hear each other. The angrier they are, the louder they will have to shout to hear each other through that great distance."

Then the saint asked, "What happens when two people fall in love? Why don't they shout at each other but talk softly? This is so because their hearts are very close. The distance between them is very small."

The saint continued, "What happens when they love each other even more? When that happens, they do not speak, only whisper, and they come even closer to each other in their love. Finally, they need not whisper; they only look at each other and understand. That is how close two people are when they love each other."

When you argue, do not let your hearts become distant. Do not say words that create distance.

94. Sunflowers

It was Monday morning. Miss Catherine welcomed the class with a bright smile and said, "Today, let me tell you something about the beautiful sunflowers. Sunflowers turn according to the position of the sun. In other words, they 'chase the light'. You might already know this, but there is another fact you probably do not know. Have you ever wondered what happens on cloudy and rainy days when the sun is completely covered by clouds?"

This is an interesting question, isn't it? Perhaps you think the sunflower withers or turns its head towards the ground. Is this what crossed your mind? Well, that's incorrect.

Catherine continued, "What actually happens is that they turn towards each other to share their energy. Nature's perfection is amazing!"

The class was stunned!

Now let's apply this reflection to our lives. Many people may become low-spirited, and the most vulnerable ones sometimes become depressed.

How about following the example of the beautiful sunflowers, i.e., 'supporting and empowering each other'?

Daffodils behave in a similar way. Nature has so much to teach us.

Wishing everyone a 'sunflower' trait of turning towards each other on their cloudy and gloomy days.

Be the sunflower, and be each other's light.

95. The Two Wolves

An old man sat down to teach his grandson about life. "There's a fight going on inside me," he said to the young boy, "a fight between two wolves. One wolf is evil. It's full of malice, anger, greed, self-pity, and false pride. The other is good. It's full of peace, love, joy, kindness, and humility. This same fight is going on inside you and everyone else on the face of the earth."

The grandson was quiet, pondering this revelation for a moment before asking, "Grandfather, which wolf will win?"

The old man smiled and replied, "The one you feed."

Good and evil exist within each of us. It's our responsibility to own that reality and do whatever we can to nurture the good.

The one you feed wins.

96. How to be 'Me-sponsible'

Andrea once shared the biggest lesson her mother taught her. Her mother had trouble sleeping. She felt exhausted. She was irritable, grumpy, and bitter. She was always sick until one day, suddenly, she changed.

One day, her father said to her mother, "I've been looking for a job for three months but haven't found anything. I'm going to have a few beers with friends."

Her mother replied, "It's okay."

Her brother said to her mother, "Mom, I'm doing poorly in all subjects at the university."

Her mother replied, "It's okay. You will recover, and if you don't, repeat the semester but pay the fee."

Her sister said to her mother, "Mom, I smashed the car."

Her mother replied, "Okay, daughter, take it to the car shop and find a way to pay for it, and while they fix it, get around by bus or subway."

These reactions were unheard of as far as Andrea's mother was concerned. They all found it unbelievable and were worried about these reactions from her. They suspected she had gone to the doctor and was prescribed some pills called 'I don't care'. Perhaps she was overdosing on those!

But then, she gathered them all around her and explained, "It took me a long time to realize that each person is responsible for their life. It took me years to discover that my anguish, anxiety, depression, courage, insomnia, and stress do not solve your problems but aggravate mine.

"I am not responsible for the actions of anyone, and it's not my job to provide happiness, but I am responsible for my reactions.

Therefore, I came to the conclusion that my duty to myself is to remain calm and let each one of you solve what corresponds to you. I can only give you my advice if you ask me, and it depends on you whether to follow it or not. There are consequences, good or bad, to your decisions, and YOU have to live with them. So, from now on, I cease to be the receptacle of your responsibilities, the sack of your guilt, the laundress of your remorse, the advocate of your faults, the wall of your lamentations, and the depositary of your duties, who should solve your problems or spare a tyre every time to fulfil your responsibilities! From now on, I declare you all independent and self-sufficient adults."

Andrea and her family were dumbfounded by the depth and veracity of their mother's words!

For some of us, this is hard because we've grown up being caregivers and feeling responsible for others. At times, we are fixers of all things. We never want our loved ones to go through difficult situations or to struggle. We want everyone to be happy, but the sooner we take that responsibility off our shoulders and onto each loved one's, the better we are preparing them to be 'Me-sponsible'.

We are not here on earth to be everything to everyone. Stop putting that pressure on yourself.

97. Dream Interpreter

A king once dreamt that he had lost all his dreams. Eager to learn what his weird dream meant, he summoned the kingdom's two best dream interpreters to decipher his dream's meaning.

The first man said the dream foretold that all of the royal family would die, and he would be left alone. Hearing this, the king had the guards punish the man for such a terrible interpretation.

The second man was sharp-witted and had witnessed the fate of the first one. He told the king that the dream meant that he wouid live longer than the royal family. The king was delighted to hear this and presented him with gifts.

The interpretation of the second man was no different from that of the first one. They meant the same thing—that the royal family would perish, leaving the king alone. But while the king punished the first dream interpreter, the second man was showered with treasured gifts.

The same message can be delivered in many ways. It is essential to learn to communicate correctly. It is not always about what you say but also how you say it.

Remember, if you can't say something nice, at least say it nicely.

98. Teacher or President?

This is a moving incident from the life of the great American author, James Michener. He had the rare privilege of being invited to be a guest at a banquet hosted by President Dwight Eisenhower at the White House.

James Michener declined the invitation. In his letter to the President, he explained, "A wonderful teacher who taught me how to write is being honoured on the same day, at the same time. You will not miss me at your banquet, Mr President, but she might, at hers."

'Ike' (as Eisenhower was popularly known) was so moved that he wrote back: "Dear Mr Michener, in his lifetime, a man lives under 15 or 16 Presidents, but a truly fine teacher comes in his lifetime far too rarely."

We often take people close to us for granted. When was the last time we appreciated, recognized, and rewarded all the people who took care of us, taught us, guided us, and helped us?

Sometimes we forget to let people know we treasure them the most.

99. Destroying and Rebuilding

Once, Ashka was invited to visit the site of a Zen Buddhist temple. When she reached there, she was surprised to see that the extraordinarily beautiful building, which was situated in the middle of a vast forest, was right next to a huge piece of wasteland. She asked what the waste ground was for, and the man in charge explained, "That is where we will build the next temple. Every 20 years, we destroy the temple you see before you now and rebuild it on the site next to it. This means that the monks who have trained as carpenters, stonemasons, and architects are always using their practical skills and passing them on to their apprentices. It also shows them that nothing in this life is eternal, and that even temples are in need of constant improvement."

Ashka was left pondering the depth of what she had heard.

Change is the only constant.

100. Helpless Love

Once upon a time, all feelings and emotions went to a coastal island for a vacation. According to their nature, each was having a good time. Suddenly, a warning of an impending storm was announced, and everyone was advised to evacuate the island.

The announcement caused sudden panic. Everyone rushed to their boats. Even damaged boats were quickly repaired and commissioned for duty. Yet, Love did not wish to flee. There was so much to do. But as the clouds darkened, Love realized it was time to leave. Alas, there were no boats to spare. Love looked around with hope.

Just then, Prosperity passed by in a luxurious boat. Love shouted, "Prosperity, could you please take me in your boat?"

"No," replied Prosperity, "my boat is full of precious possessions, gold, and silver. There is no place for you."

A little later, Vanity came by in a beautiful boat. Again, Love shouted, "Could you help me, Vanity? I am stranded and need a lift. Please take me with you."

Vanity responded haughtily, "No, I cannot take you with me. My boat will get soiled by your muddy feet."

Sorrow passed by after some time. Again, Love asked for help, but to no avail. "No, I cannot take you with me," Sorrow said. "I am so sad. I want to be by myself."

When Happiness passed by a few minutes later, Love again called for help. But Happiness was so happy that it was hardly concerned about anyone and did not look around.

Love was growing restless and dejected. Just then, somebody called out, "Come, Love, I will take you with me." Love did not know who was being so magnanimous but jumped onto the boat, greatly relieved that it would reach a safe place. On getting off the boat, Love met Knowledge. Puzzled, Love inquired, "Knowledge, do you know who so generously gave me a lift when no one else wished to help?"

Knowledge smiled, "Oh, that was Time."

"And why would Time stop to pick me and take me to safety?" Love wondered.

Knowledge smiled and replied, "Because only Time knows your true greatness and what you are capable of. Only Love can bring peace and great happiness in this world."

The important message here is that when we are prosperous, we overlook love. When we feel important, we forget love. Even in happiness and sorrow, we forget love. Only with time do we realize the importance of love.

Why wait that long? Why not make love a part of your life today?

Let there be love always.

101. Priority Check

A woman bought a parrot from a pet shop to keep her company, but she returned it the next day. "This bird doesn't talk," she told the shop owner.

"Does he have a mirror in his cage?" the store owner asked. "Parrots love mirrors. They see their reflection and start a conversation."

The woman bought a mirror and left. However, the next day, she returned. The bird still wasn't talking.

"How about a ladder? Parrots love ladders. A happy parrot is a talkative parrot," said the owner.

The woman bought a ladder and left. But the next day, she was back.

"Does he have a swing? No? Well, that's the problem. Once he starts swinging, he'll talk up a storm."

The woman reluctantly bought a swing and left. When she walked into the store the next day, her countenance had changed.

"The parrot died," she said.

The pet store owner was shocked. "I'm so sorry. Tell me, did he ever say anything?" he asked.

"Yes, right before he died," the woman replied. "In a weak voice, he asked me, 'Don't they sell any food at that pet store?'"

Sometimes we forget what's truly important in life. We get caught up in things that look good and neglect the things that are truly necessary. Take a moment to do a 'priority check', and strive for what is most important today.

Prioritize what truly matters.

My Inspiration – *Param Pujya* Pappaji: Shree Prem Acharyaji

Pappaji is a luminary figure who has left an indelible mark on many lives. From being a successful industrialist to evolving into a spiritual philosopher, Pappaji life journey serves as a profound inspiration for all those fortunate enough to have known or crossed paths with him.

What sets him apart is his objectivity amidst his conviction in the veracity of subjectivity, making him a beloved mentor among youngsters. Those blessed with his presence found themselves uplifted by his love, for he communicated not based on his own perspective but according to the individual's needs.

He founded the Asiatic Group of companies in 1955 at the young age of 25, when he started India's first factory to manufacture zinc chloride in Kolkata. His vision and business acumen directed the expansion of the business, raising the company's manufacturing facilities to 11 factories across the country. He introduced his innovation of special battery-grade 'ZINC CHLORIDE' to several European companies, and Asiatic Chemicals emerged as the sole supplier to leading dry-cell battery manufacturers in India, enjoying a monopoly for 40 years.

Having risen from humble beginnings to reach the pinnacle of success, Pappaji left everything behind and arrived in Mumbai, driven by a desire to verify whether his achievements were a result of talent, hard work, or simply luck. The deep contemplation of his success unveiled his spiritual side.

Shree Prem Acharyaji, not one to believe in religion blindly, put himself to several tests and believed in things only after experimenting. He realized that Lord Mahavir's identity for the past 2000 years has unfortunately been confined to the 24th Tirthankara, and his scriptures have largely appealed only to Jains across the globe.

Shree Prem Acharyaji munificently made the appeal that the research of Self-realized Souls is universally applicable and can be the source of divine peace for everyone. He reiterated that the universal and scientific findings of Mahavir should not be the proprietary right of a select few, and the rest of the world should not remain deprived of this great soul's purest influence.

His profound knowledge of 'karma science' made him a highly revered spiritual soul. Shree Prem Acharyaji's timeless contribution to the world is seen in the re-awakening of 'Vitraag Vigyaan', which has helped many experience the depths of silence, bliss, and peace. Despite this unique *Kshayopsham* (thinking power), he did not encourage blind faith but inspired seekers to think, experience, and then develop their belief in the philosophy.

Fearlessly embracing the truth, he dared to delve into uncharted territories. While advising young people to prioritize their careers and prove themselves, he also guided them towards an authentic path, silently igniting a spark of magic within them. Positive and creative thinking was his forte, complemented by a remarkable sense of humour and boundless love.

A truly insightful personality, he is an inspiration to the modern generation in harmonizing the materialistic and spiritual worlds. He sowed the seed of Shrimad Rajchandra Aatma Tatva Research Centre (SRATRC) to promote the universal message of self-liberation through Vitraag Vigyaan for self-realization.

How Pappaji Turned My Life Around

Dear Reader,

Where do I even start? I am glad you have completed your journey through the pages of this book and are here to delve deeper into the realm of our beloved Pappaji and the magnificent SRATRC.

As I reflect on my discovery of this magical place, I feel it was divine intervention that made me stumble upon SRATRC and cross paths with Pappaji. I, Bhawna Agrawal, was formerly Bhawna Duggar, hailing from a conventional and more or less conservative Jain family, who chose to marry the man of her dreams from the Agrawal community. This itself proves that it was the collision of two very different worlds. Add to it the fact that this world belonged to me, who has the 'WHY' Syndrome, meaning that I questioned everything around me and was restless, for there were no answers, only instructions, suggestions, orders, compulsions, and disagreements. I am extremely lucky to have the most amazing, lovable, and incredibly supportive in-laws, and I thank Pappaji and SRATRC for aiding me in realizing this. For a girl, embracing a new life after marriage is always full of challenges, and it was no different for me. However, being a part of SRATRC made me aware of my blessings. I have even authored the book, *Happily Ever After With In-Laws,* presenting a journey that is extremely close to my heart. I had questions about the rituals I had observed from childhood and also about the ones I was expected to follow after marriage, but no one liked the idea of being questioned about the same. I came across SRATRC, where I found the freedom to ask, the freedom to question my beliefs, and the freedom and encouragement to pursue my journey of

discovery, which was filled with trials and errors, confusions and doubts. To my surprise, it was all happily accepted.

My experiences, learnings, and takeaways are so many and profound that they cannot be expressed in mere words. All I can say is that the teachings of Pappaji and the way of life learnt at SRATRC have transformed me into my better version, and I am headed towards being the best version of myself.

I have been enriched as a girl, daughter, daughter-in-law, sister, sister-in-law, wife, mother, and professional—in all, as a human being.

I have evolved from being a person who feared disappointing people and being disappointed by them to someone who knows none of us has the power to do so, as each individual is responsible for their own happiness and disappointments. When I say this, I do not quote or reiterate some text from a scripture; instead, I speak from experience. Being associated with SRATRC, I have learnt to accept more and expect less. I have learnt to be a giver before being a receiver. I have learnt that the one who takes care of other people's well-being and happiness never runs short on their stock of ecstasy. I have learnt what being positive and creative truly means. I have learnt to embrace my flaws and hone my strengths. I know when I persevere, miracles are bound to manifest.